NATURE'S PARADISE

By the same author

GROWING UP WITH ANIMALS

NATURE'S PARADISE

Jen and Des Bartlett

Houghton Mifflin Company

Boston 1967

First Printing

© *Jen and Des Bartlett, 1967*

All rights reserved including the right to reproduce
this book or parts thereof in any form

Library of Congress Catalog Card Number: 66–19834

Printed and bound in Switzerland
by Conzett & Huber, Zurich

We dedicate this book to

ARMAND AND MICHAELA DENIS

with whom we have worked for ten happy years in Africa. They have made it possible for us to visit many countries since 1952 and we have shared together many pleasant and exciting moments, as well as much hard work. We hope that this book will reflect their deep concern for wildlife conservation as well as our own.

Foreword

Soestdijk, July 15th 1966

In recent years many admirable books have been inspired by the wildlife and scenery of Africa, but here is one that stands supreme. As a photographic study of a spectacular continent it is unsurpassed. As a brilliant exposition of the way in which the mammals, birds, insects, fish and reptiles of Africa are dependent on their habitat and on each other it is fascinating and unique.

Mr Bartlett has unrivalled skill and experience as a photographer of wildlife and is also an excellent field naturalist. This book records for posterity the natural treasures of one of the areas of the world where wildlife is still truly wild—a record of treasures as precious and important as the gothic cathedrals, paintings and sculptures of Europe, but with one important difference: whereas man guards and preserves his own creations, wildlife and the wild places where they live are under a constant threat of irrevocable destruction.

In reading and looking at this remarkable book we should remember and mark well the words of the late King George VI: "The wildlife of today is not ours to dispose of as we please. We have it in trust and must account for it to those who come after."

H. R. H. PRINCE BERNHARD OF THE NETHERLANDS
President, The World Wildlife Fund

Contents

Acknowledgement

This book was made possible by the foresight of devoted men and women who have worked for many years to preserve the magnificent wildlife of Africa. Countless others are today carrying on this worthwhile objective, including the authors' many friends in the National Parks and Game Departments of Kenya, Uganda, Tanzania, Zambia, Rhodesia and South Africa. On behalf of all lovers of wildlife we thank them.

Many people have helped either directly or indirectly in the preparation of this book. Chief among them has been Captain Charles Pitman, who has spent a great many hours studying the original photographic layout and checking both the text and the captions. We appreciate and value his many helpful suggestions.

We are also grateful for their help to Bob Campbell, "Musa" Quraishy, John Williams, Bob Carcasson, David Roberts, Raymond Hook, Richard Leakey, "Matt" Matthews, Geof Mason Smith, Dennis Gower, Stephen Ellis, David Sheldrick, Dave McCabe, Tony McGuire, Alan Root, Charles Cordier, Ernie Hanmer, Frank Poppleton, Myles Turner, Ted Davison, Bruce Austen, Harry Cantle, "Jordie" Jordaan, John Posselt, Rupert Fothergill, "Tinkey" Haslam, Dr. Walter Stark and William Stephens.

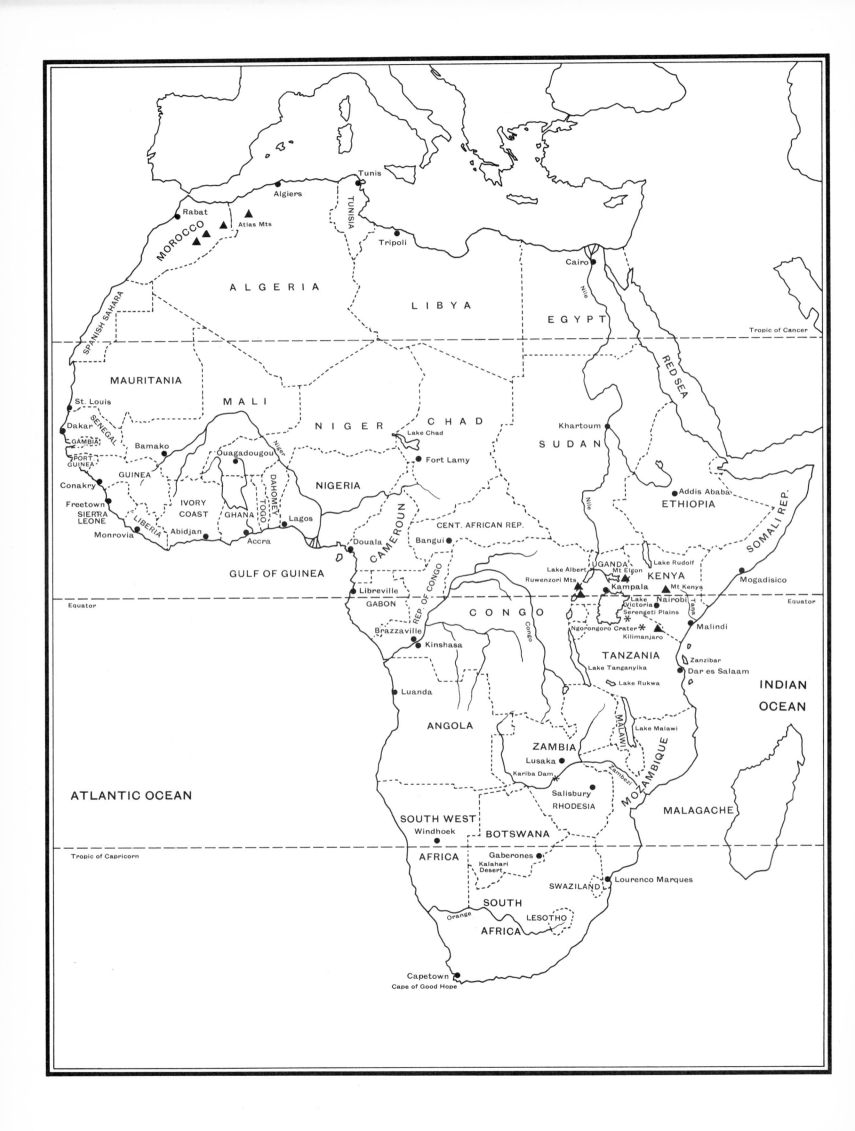

1 The Coral Reef

When Africa is mentioned people invariably visualize elephants or lions, giving little, if any, thought to the fabulous variety of creatures found along the coast. But the earliest-known forms of life dwelt in the ancient seas and the inhabitants of the sea today are no less interesting than those found on land. This even applies to Africa, where there is such a wealth of wildlife.

More than two-thirds of the earth's surface is covered by ocean, and the study of marine life is a vast field with new and surprising discoveries being made almost daily. The most rewarding and easily accessible areas for observing life under the sea are among the coral reefs of the world. Coral will flourish only in seas where the water temperature exceeds 70° F, and therefore living reefs are found only in tropical regions, roughly between the tropics of Capricorn and Cancer. Even within these latitudes coral reefs are not found off the western shores of the great land masses, as cold currents sweeping close to shore greatly reduce the water temperature. Africa has a cold Atlantic current sweeping up its west coast from the Antarctic, but to the east the warm Indian Ocean and the Red Sea provide perfect conditions for the growth of corals.

Many different reef-building organisms flourish in fairly shallow water where sunlight penetrates, and although the individual living creatures are often tiny they cluster together in their millions. The minute marine animals known as coral polyps live in colonies which look like flowers when their tentacles are extended to feed. Every polyp secretes a supporting cup of lime as it grows, a stony skeleton that it leaves behind when it dies. New polyps continually grow outwards from the main colony, and in this way a reef may grow an inch in height during a year. Living corals cannot exist for long out of water so that any part of a reef exposed for lengthy periods at low tide will consist of only dead corals. But this limestone fortress makes an ideal home for a countless multitude of other living creatures, and a reef is therefore never entirely dead, even when the surface coral polyps have died.

The coral reef along the east coast of Africa is known as a fringing reef. In most places it is only a few hundred yards from shore and easily approached at low tide. Between the reef and the shore there is a channel of deeper water sheltered from the pounding waves of the Indian Ocean. From the air this can be seen clearly for the waves break on the reef and not along the shoreline. In the sheltered lagoon a great variety of tropical reef fish, sea urchins, starfish and shellfish mingle in a garden of colour.

Binoculars are needed to study mammals and birds in close detail, but a simple glass-fronted face mask opens up a new world for anyone visiting a coral reef. Many people fail to explore a reef because they are not expert at swimming and diving. This should not prevent them from using a mask, as few experiences can be more rewarding than looking underwater for the first time. At low tide expanses of the reef are exposed. Amongst the coral outcrops there are many pools of crystal-clear water, often only a foot or two deep. These pools frequently have a white sandy bottom which reflects light into the nooks and crannies of the surrounding reef. To lie partly submerged in the warm tropical water is like a visit to paradise, such is the beauty and the blending of brilliant colours in this underwater fairyland. Fish and other creatures flee to safety at one's approach, but if one lies quietly in the water they quickly lose their initial fear—first staring out from the protecting branches of the coral, and then swimming out to investigate the human visitor in their midst.

The living coral formations grow in different shapes and colours, resembling an undersea garden where the prettiest plants and flowers are actually forms of animal life. The coral creates not only the "trees" of the reef, but also the hills, mountains, valleys and caves. The coral polyps feed mainly at night, when zooplankton is concentrated towards the surface of the ocean. The polyps extend numerous tentacles, each equipped with poisonous stinging cells capable of paralyzing the small prey floating in the water. Sticky threads ensnare the immobilized victims, while the tentacles draw the food into the central mouth opening. The colourful tentacles are like the petals of flowers as they sway back and forth in the ever-changing currents surging around the reef. Some kinds of coral are long, thin, and branched like the antlers of elk and other species of deer; others grow in delicately thin folds like a shawl. Brain corals resemble giant boulders many feet across, with the surface ribbed in patterns like the brain of an animal.

The fish of the reef are living jewels, though the colours soon fade if the fish are caught and taken out of the water. Perhaps the most majestic of all is the fabulous moorish idol, shaded with black, white, blue and yellow, and with a tremendously elongated dorsal fin curving above its back like a streamer. Off the coast of Kenya it is often possible to see over a dozen of these beauties together, swimming sedately about with equally brilliant tangs, demoiselles and butterfly fish. If pursued they will quickly disappear under an overhang of coral, flattening themselves against the back surface of the cave without moving. There are many species of butterfly fish, all attractively marked and often brightly coloured. Some butterfly fish have false eye spots near the tail, while the real eye is disguised by a broad dark line. This undoubtedly serves to mislead any predator into attacking the wrong end of the fish. (False eye spots also occur among a number of different insects.)

The brilliantly coloured parrotfish move across the reef in schools, and it is possible to hear them eating as they crunch the living coral in their strong beak-like mouths. They owe their name to their beaks, but their colouring is every bit as gaudy as that of their namesakes.

Numerous species of fish use the coral as a fortress into which they can instantly retreat at the first sign of danger. Many types of demoiselles or damsel fish live amongst the coral, their brilliant colours aflame as they appear to dance in and out amongst the stony branches. So small are some that over a hundred may be clustered within the protecting prongs of a single coral formation only a foot in diameter.

Other fish do not need to hide amongst coral for protection as they have their own built-in defence. Using an unusual method to avoid death, the family of puffer fish can greatly increase their size by inflating their bodies with either air or water when threatened; and because of toxic substances within their bodies they are seldom eaten by larger fish. The porcupine fish is even more highly specialized, as it becomes a veritable pincushion when inflated; its sharp spines stick out in every direction and deter even the hungriest enemy.

The different species of scorpion fish (which are also called dragon fish, butterfly cod, zebra fish, turkey fish and many other common names) are protected by venom just as deadly as that of a snake. The sharp dorsal spines are hollow like a hypodermic needle, and venom can be instantly ejected from poison sacs at their base should the fish be seized by an enemy. Even a mild "sting" from a scorpion fish can produce excruciating pain, and a few people have died from encounters with them. However, the venom is for protection only, and the scorpion fish will not deliberately attack either a human or another fish. It seems to know it will not be molested and floats unconcernedly in the water without moving out of the way at one's approach. Often six or more of these striking fish will gather around a large coral outcrop, all suspended motionless in the water as if anchored by invisible threads. The pattern of various shades of reds, browns and black make it a beautiful fish, and its elongated feathery fins enable it to swim with a poetry of motion that is fascinating to watch. It has a prodigious appetite, and remains motionless in the water while waiting for a small fish to disregard its presence and swim close. It then opens its enormous mouth and sucks in water—while the little fish disappears suddenly, drawn into the gaping mouth as if by an invisible magnet.

Although the scorpion fish has venom as deadly as a snake, there are actually water snakes living on the reefs. The poison of some species is even more deadly than that of land snakes, but on the whole they are very shy and move swiftly out of the way at one's approach. Moray eels look like snakes, but are in fact strangely developed fish. They peer out from holes in the reef with large mouths agape, showing off a formidable set of needle-sharp teeth. Although they are not venomous their bite is extremely painful, taking a long time to heal. Morays always look aggressive but usually do not attack unless approached too closely. Another fish living on the reef has an elongated, snake-like body, although it is only about six inches long. This is the delicate little pipefish, a relative of the seahorse. The female lays her eggs into the brood pouch of the male. In a few weeks fifty or more babies have fully developed within the long pouch. Its walls then open, and the thread-like young pipefish begin life on their own.

There are many colourful creatures which are not fish even though their common name includes the word "fish". Starfish, or sea stars as they are more correctly called, are often brilliantly coloured. They vary greatly in shape from the large pincushion stars, which are almost round with only slight points indicating the ends of the five arms, to the brittle stars which have very slender and agile arms. These brittle stars move in the sinuous fashion of a snake, hence their other common name of serpent stars. The sea urchins are related to the starfish, even though their round, spine-covered bodies look totally different. Both the starfish and the sea urchin move about by using small tube feet which can be extended; suction discs at the end of the feet then grip solid objects in order to pull the creature along. Although each tube foot is quite small there are literally dozens of them, and the combined force which they can exert is considerable. The starfish is carnivorous, living on bivalves—shellfish which have two similar shells hinged together by a very strong muscle. So strong is this muscle that a man cannot force the two shells apart, yet a starfish manages to do so. The secret of its success lies in its endurance. Its tube feet strain to pull the two shells open, but for a time they remain tightly closed. Undaunted, the starfish maintains its pull until the bivalve slowly tires, enabling the starfish to begin a leisurely meal.

With patience, the underwater observer will be able to see many of the smaller creatures and to witness many strange relationships. Perhaps the strangest home of all for a fish is among the stinging tentacles of a sea anemone. The flower-like sea anemones are related to the corals and are also carnivorous. They do not live on microscopic organisms in the water but can catch and digest small fish. Their many tentacles are covered with tiny stinging cells which release poison darts on contact. However, clown fish are evidently immune. They seem to delight in rubbing themselves deep among the tentacles of the anemone in the way a cat rubs itself against a person's leg. It is as if they are indicating to other fish that this is a perfectly safe place to hide. But if another small fish does swim against the tentacles it is stung and caught, and then drawn into the centrally located digestive chamber of the anemone.

As an experiment we tried feeding pieces of fish to some clown fish living with a giant anemone. Each time, a clown fish would swim out to catch the slowly sinking piece of fish meat in its mouth; but instead of eating this itself the fish would swim back to deposit the prize near the centre of the anemone. It was fascinating to see the clown fish actually feeding the anemone. Perhaps the clown fish prefers its food partly digested by the anemone? This is an association of two unlike animals which needs more detailed study before its significance is fully understood.

Living with the same giant anemone were two little porcellanid crabs no more than an inch across. They were light in colour but finely dotted with pink. Moving about amongst the tentacles while feeding, they picked up and ate small particles of food in a normal crab fashion. However, they had another rather unusual method of gathering food. While sitting on the surface of the anemone a little porcellanid would rhythmically wave first its left "arm" then its right "arm"— each a specially developed feeding appendage—to strain microscopic plankton from the seawater. After doing this for a minute or two, it would stop to comb the catch off the feather-like gills with the next pair of small brush-tipped legs, thus transferring the collected food to its mouth.

Anemones seem to consort with a number of other creatures, no doubt associations which are mutually beneficial. Normally an anemone will remain anchored firmly to a suitable rock, even though it is capable of moving slowly to a new locality. A hermit crab will sometimes place one or two small anemones on the top of the shell it has adopted as its home. This helps to camouflage the shell, and the stinging tentacles of the anemone no doubt give some measure of protection to the crab, while the anemone benefits by being constantly on the move to new feeding grounds.

There is always something new to see, no matter how many times one has visited a reef before. Yet many fish stay in the one place month after month and one can soon learn to recognize individuals. Fish watching can become just as fascinating as bird watching. As birds congregate around a feeding table, so do fish congregate if they are fed regularly, and many soon become tame enough to feed from the hand. It is hard to imagine the pleasure derived from something as simple as this; but the fish soon become personalities, each with a different character that can be recognized. To have the trust of any wild creatures is deeply rewarding and automatically leads to their care and protection. This in turn develops into an awareness of all nature, and with such an interest life is never boring.

The waves of the Indian Ocean breaking on the coral reef along the coast of East Africa, just south of Mombasa. This reef protects the shoreline from the full fury of the waves during the monsoon seasons.

Coconut palms fringe the coastline of much of tropical Africa. Native fish traps are carefully constructed so that fish swimming along the coast encounter the stick fence and are guided by it into the circular holding pen. The fisherman can then easily collect his catch at low tide, when the water is only knee-deep.

Starfish of many shapes and colours are a common ▸ sight in the warm water of the Indian Ocean along Kenya's coastline, where living corals add beauty to the underwater scene.

The sweetlips *(Gaterin gaterinus)* is an attractive ▸▸ shallow water species of the Indo-Pacific tropics. The young of many species of reef fish are often clearly marked and vividly coloured, changing radically in appearance as they grow.

◄ A young sea bat fish *(Platax)* swims in such a way that it resembles a piece of seaweed drifting in the ocean. Irregular blotches camouflage it well, with a dark stripe breaking up the round outline of the eye.

▲ In marked contrast to the *Platax,* the striped blenny *(Runula rhinorhynchos)* is long and narrow, decorated with vivid electric blue stripes along its body. The tiny mouth is on the undersurface of its head, just forward of the eye.

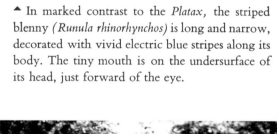

The striped blenny does not rely on camouflage, but has learnt to back into a narrow hole in a rock for a resting place, with just its head protruding. Thus it avoids predators.

23

◀◀ The colourful green and red wrasse *(Halichoeres kawarin)* buries itself in the sand when it wishes to sleep in safety at night.

▲ The spotted blenny *(Exallias brevis)* uses its pectoral fins to prop itself up amongst the coral.

◀ A goby is more at home on the bottom, resting on the sand or the weed covered rocks.

The moorish idol *(Zanclus cornutus)* is one of the ▶ most beautiful of all tropical fish, and in the Coral Gardens, off Malindi, several can be seen at the same time, swimming majestically about in the company of other brightly coloured reef fish.

When seen in the shallows at low tide these tiny ▶▶ shad *(Eucinostomus)* are almost invisible until the rays of the sun light up their scales, making them shine like polished silver.

▲ Another sharp-nosed puffer *(Canthigaster valen-tini)* is swimming in a characteristic fashion with its tail folded, the breast fins alone propelling it slowly through the water.

Flecked with white this sharp-nosed puffer ▶ *(Canthigaster margaritatus)* has a dark false eyespot which is more easily noticed than its real eye.

The porcupine fish *(Diodon holacanthus)* can quickly inflate its body with either air or water when in danger, turning itself into a pincushion of sharp spines which few fish would want to swallow.

▲ With its delicate pattern of lines and dots this young surgeon fish *(Zebrasoma)* does not look at all like the adult into which it will grow. The sharp lance, which is responsible for its common name of surgeon or doctor fish, can be seen as a white mark at the base of the tail.

Top left: the vivid colour and striking pattern of this nudibranch, or ▶ sea-slug *(Phyllidia)* contrasts greatly with the drab-coloured algae on which it is crawling. Centre left: this brilliantly coloured young wrasse *(Coris formosa)* is very active and yet has the common name of "lazy fish" owing to its habit of burying itself in the sand to sleep. Bottom left: the coachman *(Heniochus acuminatus)* looks rather like the moorish idol, shown in colour on page 27, although it is not related and its dorsal fin is not nearly as long. Top right: There are many types of sea urchins along the east coast of Africa, but few are more colourful than this species, *(Astropyga radiata)*. Centre right: the young spotted box fish *(Ostracion tuberculatus)* is an odd-looking fish with a box-like body. It moves through the water like a helicopter—tilting, turning or standing on end while hovering in one spot. Bottom right: the venomous scorpion fish *(Pterois volitans)* has many popular names such as dragon fish, feather fish, zebra fish, and turkey fish.

A coral reef is like a fortress for the vast multitude of colourful demoiselles or damsel fish. When danger threatens they vanish almost instantly only to reappear moments later peering from the protective branches of the coral growths. *Dascyllus aruanus* swims past the coral (above right) showing the three dark stripes of this species. *Dascyllus reticulatus* can be seen hiding (above left) and side on (below).

Flecked demoiselle (*Pomacentrus pavo*)

Blue demoiselle (*Abudefduf biocellatus*)

Soap cod (*Grammistes sexlineatus*)

Sailfin tang (*Zebrasoma veliferum*)

Butterfly fish (*Chaetodon lunula*)

Submarine blenny (*Runula tapeinosoma*)

◀◀ The common colour phase of the beautiful but deadly dragon fish *(Pterois volitans)*.

There are many species of scorpion fish in the Red Sea and along the tropical coast of East Africa, all attractively marked and capable of inflicting painful wounds. The points of the poison spikes are visible at the tips of the vertical dorsal spines, and these are hollow—like a hypodermic needle—with a poison sac at their base. Even a small amount of venom will cause a person to suffer horrible agony, and a number of people have died from such a sting. Two species are shown on this page—the dark colour phase of *Pterois volitans*, and *Pterois antennata* with its needle-like fins.

The stinging tentacles of a sea anemone will ▶ quickly kill most small fish on contact, but the clown fish *(Amphiprion)* can snuggle amongst the tentacles with complete immunity.

The giant sea anemone is an animal even though ▶▶ it looks more like a flower growth. Here it is giving protection to a number of small damsel fish *(Dascyllus trimaculatus)* on the left, two tiny anemone crabs (also called porcellanid crabs) and colourful clown fish *(Amphiprion)* shown in close up on the following page.

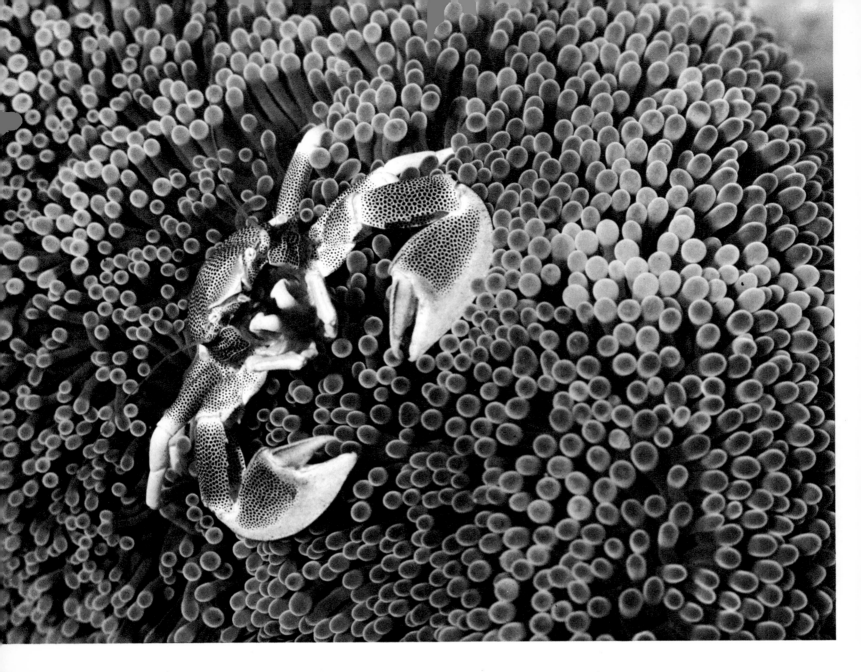

The tiny pink spotted anemone crab is only an inch across and lives safely among the stinging tentacles of the sea anemone. Each of the giant anemones we observed off the East African coast usually had two of these little porcellanid crabs living with it—also a number of colourful clown fish of different sizes, and perhaps twenty or more damsel fish. This tiny crab moves all over the anemone feeding amongst the stinging tentacles in a typical crab fashion—picking up small particles of food in its claws and transferring them to its mouth. But as these photographs show, it has a pair of specially adapted legs, or feeding appendages, equipped with retractable "combs", and these are alternately swept, in a rhythmical circular motion, to strain plankton from the sea water. Tiny brushes on the next pair of legs then clean these tiny food particles from the combs before transferring them to the mouth.

◄◄ The striking appearance of a ghost crab *(Ocy-pode)* is apparent when viewed from its own level. It does most of its scavenging on the beach at night, running off like a shadowy "ghost" when disturbed.

This crab *(Calappa)* has large, spanner-like nippers which meet to protect the front of its body, hence its common name of bashful crab.

To escape predators the bashful crab is able to bury itself quickly in the wet sand, leaving just the tips of its eye stalks visible.

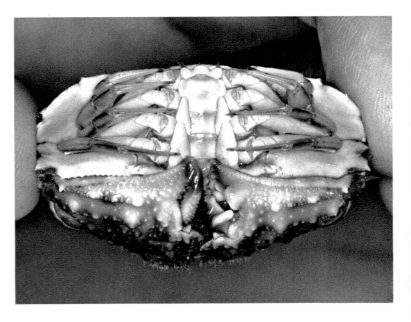

The strong shell over its back extends to overlap and adequately protect its folded legs—which can only be seen when the bashful crab is turned upside down.

This ghost crab looks like the ghost crab shown on page 46 except for its
very pointed eye stalks, which fold down to fit into the two recesses in the shell.

The terminal suckers on the tube feet, which enable the sea star or starfish to move about, can only be seen from the underside if the starfish can be persuaded to "walk" on a pane of glass. The centrally located mouth and "teeth" show clearly the close-up photograph, as well as the suckers on the tube feet.

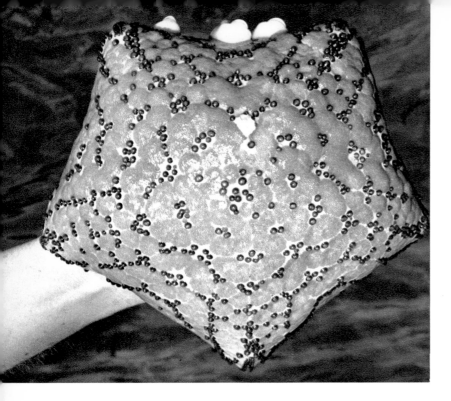 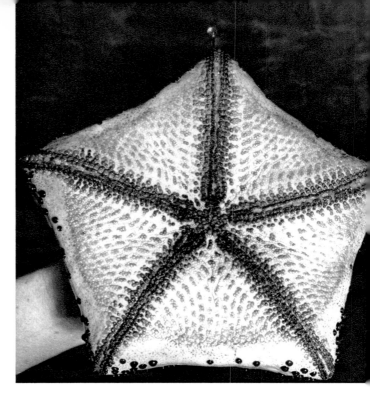

The upper and lower surfaces of another sea star which has the common name of pincushion starfish. It is able to move slowly over the sea floor by means of the tube feet which are now retracted and concealed in the five radiating slits.

The sea urchin is related to the sea stars, although its round, spine-covered body looks totally different. In this species *(Astropyga radiata)* the five body segments, equivalent to the arms of a starfish, can be clearly seen. Spiny sea urchins propel themselves by the use of long retractable tube feet which are completely hidden when not in use. The spines are also movable, and in some species can help in locomotion, as well as to wedge the sea urchin safely into the crevice of a rock.

This tube worm, or "feather duster" as it is sometimes called, lives buried vertically in the sand, with just the tip of the tube casing showing. The only parts of the worm ever visible are the feathery tentacles, or gills, which can be extended from the top of the tube to strain minute particles of food from the sea water. The two tubes shown on the hand, with the worms safely concealed inside, give an idea of their size.

The extended gills of this tube worm are actually only one inch in diameter, and the full beauty of these flower-like ▶▶ creatures cannot be fully appreciated unless greatly enlarged, as shown on the following page.

53

Spiny lobsters *(Panulirus),* or crayfish as they are often called, are plentiful along the east coast of Africa, hiding in rocky crevices during the day and moving about to feed at night.

When viewed in close-up it is easy to see why the common name of spiny lobster was given to these creatures. The rounded eyes are protected by two particularly long spines, with shorter spines extending along the carapace or shell.

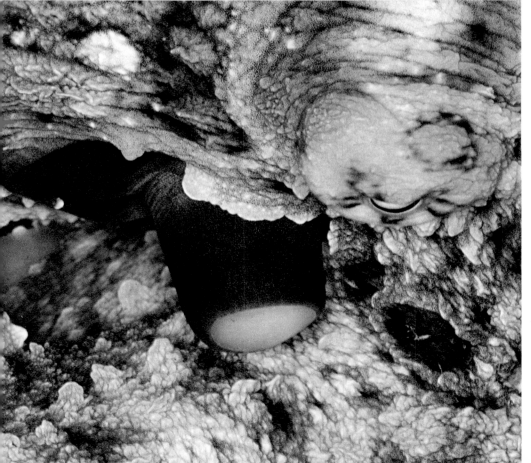

An octopus moves backwards through the sea by forcefully expelling water through its syphon—an efficient form of jet-propulsion.

In close-up the shape of the syphon can be clearly seen, and just to the front of the syphon the lidless eye can be distinguished by the dark semicircular band of the pupil.

Out of its watery element, an octopus slithers ▶▶ along on wet sand making for the sea.

The suction discs on the tentacles of an octopus ▶▶▶ have great adhesive strength. Viewed through glass the horny rim of each suction disc can be clearly seen, and also the central piston-like part which is withdrawn to create a vacuum. When an octopus refuses to release its suckers they may hold so tightly that the creature can be torn away leaving the suction discs behind.

57

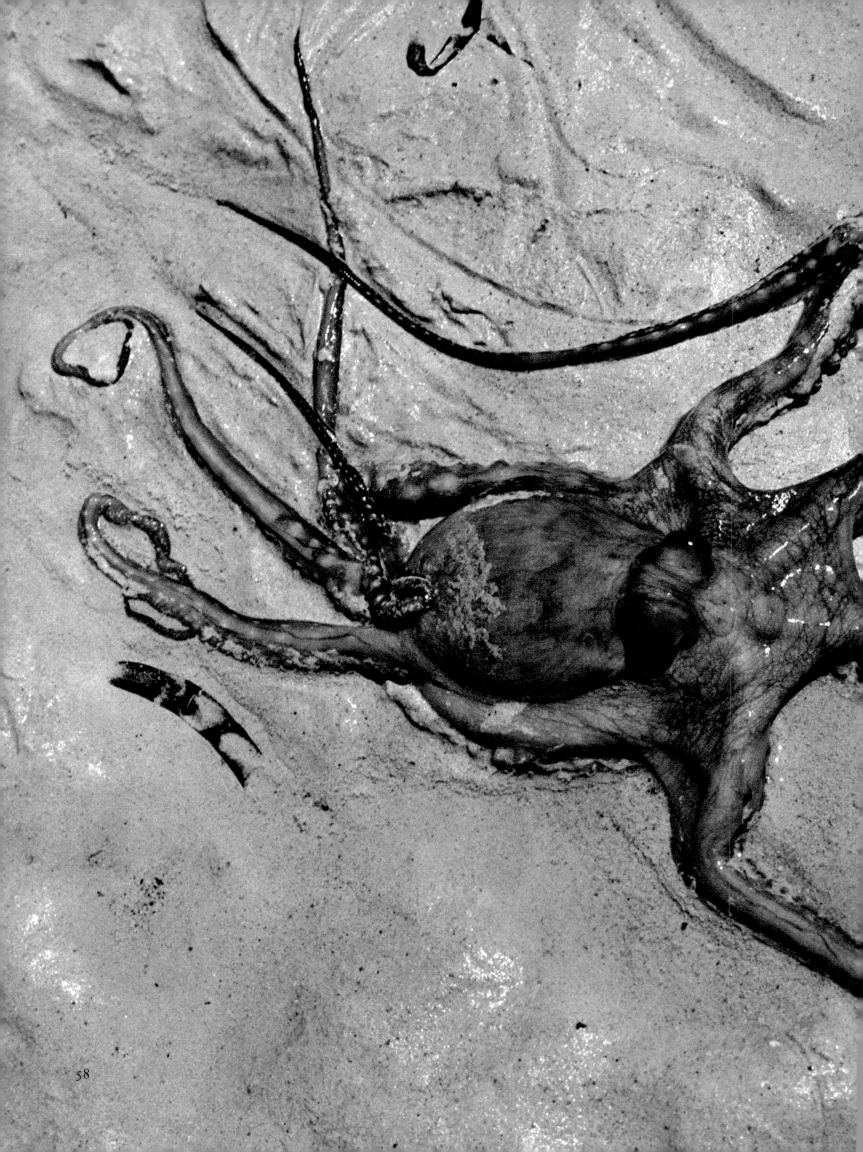

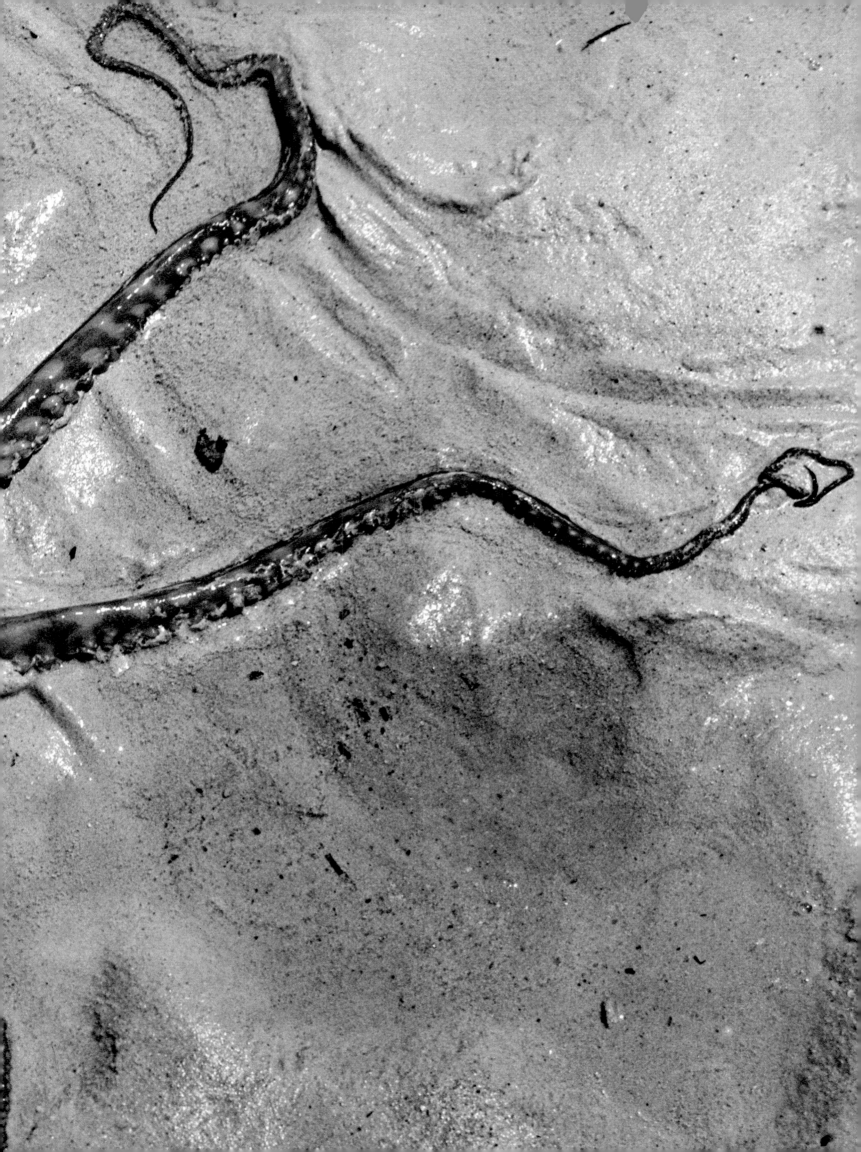

2 Dry Thornbush Country

Moving inland from the coral reef and the coastal region one enters the dry thornbush country which is typically African, stretching as it does for hundreds of miles from the west to the east coast. Between the vast Sahara Desert to the north and the equatorial rain forest belt of the Congo to the south, there is a semi-arid zone reaching from Mauretania and Senegal on the Atlantic Coast across to the Sudan in the east. The Ethiopian highlands break up this dry belt, but similar country is typical of the Somalia peninsula, projecting into the Indian Ocean and known as the Horn of Africa. Dry thornbush country is also typical of considerable areas of Kenya, Uganda and Tanzania further south. Few people who have been on a safari to East Africa would fail to think of this type of country as being "the real Africa". Although separated from the above areas by hundreds of miles of woodland country, the whole of the western side of southern Africa is semidesert; its acacia thornbush looks the same and supports many similar mammals and birds.

The dry thornbush country is therefore a feature of vast areas of Africa. Its acacias belong to a large genus of leguminous trees which thrive in areas with a rainfall of between ten and thirty inches a year. There are many species of acacia, ranging from tiny bushes to the magnificent flat-topped thorn trees fifty or sixty feet in height, with branches spreading out like an umbrella to form a crown of leaves a hundred feet or more across. It is always a wonderful sight to see a giraffe reaching up to feed on a flat-topped thorn tree: if the succulent leaves are just out of reach the giraffe's long tongue will snake out to curl round a twig, bringing the spray down into its mouth. These tall acacias are safe from other browsing animals, although the elephant can reach up with its trunk to break off whole branches in order to eat the leaves and twigs. The colour photograph on pages 74–5 shows a typical flat-topped thorn tree festooned with weaver birds' nests—the dead branches hanging down are the aftermath of a visit by elephants.

The African acacias have feathery leaves similar to many of the Australian acacia or wattle trees. Certain types of acacia have thorns four inches or more long, while those of others, popularly known as wait-a-bit thorns, are short and hooked like a rose's. The small, sweet-scented flowers resemble miniature powder puffs, varying in colour from almost white, through yellow, to a deep ochrous-orange. These delicate flowers attract many insects, particularly wasps, bees, beetles and ants. The blooms are also popular with butterflies, especially the small lycaenids or blues: some of these little living jewels frequent the flowers of just one species of acacia, their caterpillars feeding on the leaves in close association with ants living in the thorn galls. In exchange for the sweet secretion from the lycaenid caterpillars the ants protect and care for them, keeping them in their nests like a herd of domestic cows. The large blue in Great Britain has similar habits in relation to ants. Some lycaenid caterpillars do not eat the leaves of the tree, but feed on the ants' own young within the nest—a condition tolerated by the ants in exchange for the honey-dew secreted by the butterfly caterpillars.

Although dry, these areas teem with life, much of it unnoticed by the casual observer. Plants are the basis of all animal life and the hardy acacias are the main feature of the habitat. Most animals eat the living leaves, but the lowly termites live on dead wood only. They thrive here in millions, staying safely underground during the heat of the day. In the cool of the evening the workers build insulated tunnels along the surface of the ground and up the trunks of trees. Throughout the night the building work goes on. When sleeping on the ground one is not aware of this ceaseless activity; but in the morning one finds long mud trails built on the undersurface of the bottom blanket. Fortunately the termites spend the night in building only and wait until after daylight before eating the bark or the blanket, protected as they are from the sunlight and heat by their earth-walled runways.

The abundance of termites living in this type of country helps to support a variety of insects, birds and mammals which prey upon them. Although unobserved by most people, there are many insects which are savage and ruthless killers, eating more in proportion to their size than a pride of lions. Termites are the preferred food of a species of ponerine ant, and a raid by these ants is like a well-organized military operation. They are commonly called company ants because they resemble a company of soldiers in action. First, scouts are sent out from the ants' nest to find an opening to a termite tunnel. A successful scout then leads a raiding party, usually numbering between fifty and five hundred ants, which follows the scout in an orderly procession to the opening. Most of the half-inch-long ants then mill about outside while smaller raiders enter the termite home, stinging the unfortunate occupants to death. The dead termites are then carried out and dropped on the ground, the raiders returning for more victims. The larger ants outside pick up the dead termites in their big jaws, each one often carrying two or three corpses. Almost as if by a signal the raid is called off, and the heavily loaded ants return to their nest in a column three or four abreast. Some of the returning raiders carry not termites but dead and injured colleagues. Meanwhile termite workers are busily sealing off the fateful tunnel, making it useless for the ants to return for another raid.

The dry thornbush country does not, at first glance, seem to have much to offer birds in the way of food, and yet it is in many ways a bird lover's paradise. Many species of birds love to eat termites, but with the main nest underground they can catch relatively few. However, there are quite large mammals which live almost entirely on termites, and are well adapted by nature for digging out their nests. The largest termite eater is the ant-bear or aardvark, an extremely power-ful creature with a well-rounded body, long ears and snout, short stubby legs, and a tapering tail. Its strong front claws are a few inches long and it is a simple matter for the aardvark to open up a termite mound, or to dig down to an underground nest. The long, tubular tongue easily follows the twists and turns of the tunnels, and the insects sticking to its surface are greedily consumed.

Another termite and ant eater is the strange-looking pangolin. Forest-dwelling species live in trees and have long prehensile tails, while others are ground-dwelling creatures digging out under-ground nests of both termites and ants. Pangolins are well protected by overlapping scaly plates, and if threatened they roll up into a ball to protect their soft underparts. Pangolins also have long tubular tongues suited to following the termite tunnels. The hyena-like aardwolf, on the other hand, has a broad flat tongue, and yet it also lives primarily on termites. Like the aardvark and the pangolin, the aardwolf is nocturnal, and it eats the termites when they are building their surface tunnels of mud. The broad, tacky surface of the aardwolf's tongue is efficient at mopping up the scattering termites after their runways have been broken.

The spring hare is another nocturnal animal which is common in dry thornbush country in both East Africa and the Kalahari Desert area of South-West Africa. Their large eyes shine red in the headlights of a car, and when hopping off to the safety of their burrows the gleaming eyes look like tiny balls of fire bouncing along in the darkness. Spring hares live on roots and tubers, getting their entire water needs in this way.

Also feeding on roots and tubers is another animal totally different in appearance to the attractive spring hare; it is found in northern Kenya and Somalia and is rather repulsive-looking, with minute black eyes and a wrinkled pink skin, naked except for a few scattered hairs. This is the naked mole rat, a species of rodent living entirely underground and found nowhere else in the world. Tunnelling along several inches below the surface, the naked mole rat frequently needs to remove surplus loose earth from its burrow. The fine soil is flung out of a surface hole in such a way as to look like a miniature volcano erupting.

Animals living in cool underground retreats during the heat of the day can naturally conserve moisture. But living above ground in the dry thornbush country there are large herbivorous creatures which do not drink water at all, even when it is readily available. One interesting animal of this type is the gerenuk, or giraffe-necked gazelle, which can be found in northern Tanzania, Kenya and Somalia. An agile, delicate-looking antelope, with long slender legs and neck, it is pinkish-fawn in colour, the males only having lyre-shaped horns. Living on the leaves of bushes, it is particularly fond of various species of acacia. Being an expert browser, the gerenuk has learnt to stand on its hind legs to eat leaves which would otherwise be well out of its reach.

Another antelope which does not need to drink water is the diminutive dik dik, which is well adapted to life in dry thornbush country. In certain areas dik diks are very common, but they only associate in small family parties of a male and female, with perhaps one offspring. At birth a dik dik weighs in the region of one pound, and when fully grown only about ten pounds. Each family has its own territory, marked in a number of spots by well-used dung heaps. There is an amusing native legend about this habit. One day a dik dik was chased by a lion, and it was just managing to keep ahead. But looking behind to see if the lion was gaining, the dik dik suddenly fell over the large droppings of a rhinoceros. Since that day, long ago, the dik diks always use a communal dung heap in the hope of one day tripping a rhino.

Apart from the mammals which are totally independent of water, there are many species which live only within range of permanent water. Vervet monkeys will frequent the trees growing along a river, whereas baboons will move out across the ground during the day in search of food—returning to sleep in the large riverine trees at night. Antelopes differ in their ability to move away from water: impala inhabit dry thornbush country but do not range very far from a supply. Other species, like Grant's gazelle and oryx antelope, can live in dry territory well away from water although they will drink when it is available.

The carnivores are restricted to areas where water is available, but lions, leopards, caracals, hyenas and mongooses do live in the dry thornbush country. Lions may hunt many miles from water, but after a meal they like to have a drink before lying down in the shade to sleep. During a drought they find life relatively easy as more and more waterholes dry up, forcing the herbivores to concentrate around the remaining water. Species like the gerenuk, which do not have to drink, have a definite survival advantage over antelope such as the impala which cannot venture many miles from water, and are therefore often ambushed while drinking. Nevertheless, the impala is a hardy species and, where it is protected from the ravages of man, is increasing in numbers and extending its range despite natural predation.

Even large animals differ greatly in their ability to range away from water. Close to a permanent waterhole all the edible vegetation is soon eaten during a drought, and therefore many animals may starve to death even if there is ample water available. During the severe drought in East Africa of 1961 about two hundred black rhinoceroses died in the Tsavo National Park through malnutrition, even though they stayed close to water. Elephants, on the other hand, could travel a much greater distance from water, and were therefore able to find enough vegetation to survive.

After rain the acacias flower, later producing a prolific crop of seeds contained in spirally twisted pods, which are greatly relished by many animals. An elephant sometimes shakes the trunk of a large acacia tree to dislodge the ripening seed pods, and then moves slowly round picking them up with its trunk. When it has eaten the last one on the ground it will move back to give the tree another series of shakes.

Although the acacia seeds are eaten by a variety of animals, many pods remain on the trees to ripen and split, scattering the seeds on the ground below. Here they are quickly buried beneath the loose sandy soil, well protected from drying out by a hard outer case. Many species of dove, sparrow and weaver thrive on thorn tree seeds, and soon those on the surface are all eaten. The hornbills are expert diggers, moving their beaks back and forth rhythmically through the loose soil. The smaller seed eaters such as weavers and sparrows often capitalize on this, flying down to surround a foraging hornbill. As seeds are uncovered the quick little birds hop in to snatch up the prize, but this does not seem to upset the hornbill. It carries on working, soon getting plenty of seeds and grubs for itself—picking each one up in the tip of its long beak, tossing it into the air, and swallowing it in one gulp.

It is fascinating to study how the lives of plants, insects, birds and mammals in the dry thornbush country tie in together. Some species, such as the naked mole rat, have a limited range, while others are very adaptable. The elephant is perhaps the best example of this: it is equally at home in the dry thornbush, in open woodlands and in thick rain forests. Elephants live happily near the coast at sea level and yet are also found on high mountain ranges where they sometimes venture to a height of 14,000 feet. Even though persecuted by man for centuries, they are so adaptable that they are not threatened with extinction. But the creatures which cannot adapt from one habitat to another are the ones which need careful watching; comprehensive government policies are required to safeguard their environment, which is just as important as protecting the animals themselves.

Limitless distance and no sign of human habitation make this a typical dry thornbush scene in Africa, with the build up of clouds heralding the approach of the short rainy season.

In semidesert country termite mounds are often a ▶ colourful feature of the landscape. The number of termites living in each acre of open country defies the imagination, but must run into countless millions.

The queen termite is nothing more than an egg-laying machine lying in the royal Chamber and constantly attended by a procession of workers. The large white object, four inches long, is her greatly distended abdomen, her tiny head and thorax being partly hidden by the workers who continuously attend her every need, as she is totally incapable of locomotion.

Somehow the lowly termites know of the approach of the wet season, and the workers—guarded by the larger warriors—start building up the ventilation shafts to prevent flooding of the underground nest. ▼

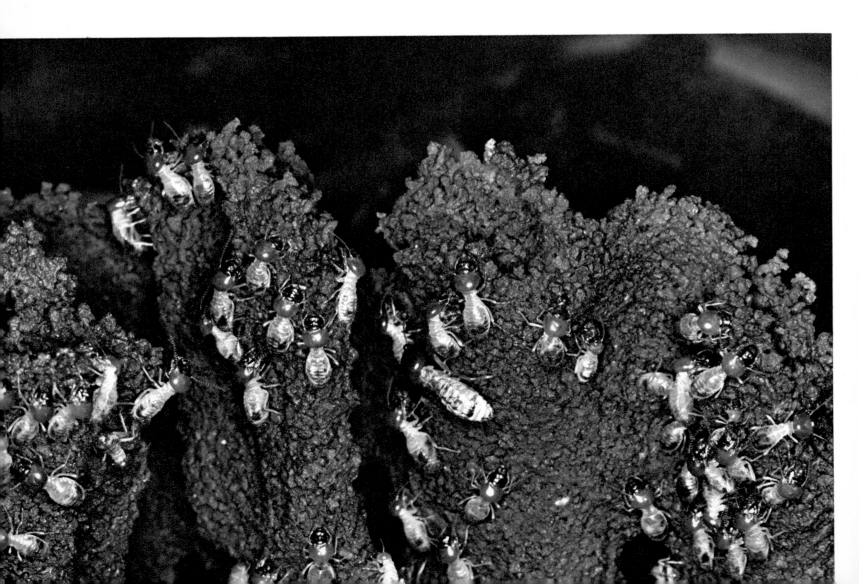

As mentioned in the text the termites are raided by many other creatures, especially by the highly organized ponerine ants seen here returning from a raid with termites clutched firmly in their jaws.

Many species of birds live on insects, and termites are often a favourite food. The red-billed horn-bill calling from an acacia tree is often seen hopping about on the ground in search of insects.

Another eater of termites is the superb glossy starling. It is one of Africa's most beautiful birds, and around permanent camps in game country these birds become very tame, often flying onto tables in search of crumbs.

A number of animals feed almost entirely on termites, frequenting dry thornbush country where those insects are plentiful. The largest termite eater is the aardvark, which has a very strong and muscular body weighing 150 pounds or more.

Another termite and ant eater is the strange-looking pangolin, which walks balanced on its hind legs with the long tail held out behind, effectively counter-balancing the weight of its head and body. When frightened the pangolin rolls itself into a ball with its tail curled round to protect the soft underside of its body and its head. The hard overlapping plates are all that can be seen from the outside.

Aardwolfs feed almost entirely on termites and live in underground burrows which they excavate themselves. They usually lead a solitary existence, but during the breeding season the youngsters remain with the mother until quite large. The father does not share the same burrow. Very few people have ever seen a baby aardwolf, but few animals are more appealing. When small, they make a clicking sound which is very similar to the warning sound made by termites.

◀◀ The flat-topped thorn tree (previous page), often festooned with weaver birds' nests, is a typical feature of the African dry country landscape. Only giraffe and elephant are tall enough to feed on these high leaves, and the hanging branches indicate that elephants have browsed here.

The bold pattern of the reticulated giraffe makes it a favourite for exhibition in zoological gardens. Large herds of seventy to a hundred or more are still sometimes seen in Northern Kenya. Opposite is a Masai giraffe stretching to reach the high leaves of a yellow thorn tree.

The reticulated giraffe shares the open thornbush country north of the Equator with the finely marked Grevy's zebras. Although living in the same habitat the giraffe browse on acacia and other trees while the Grevy's zebras feed on the grasses underneath.

The Grevy's is the largest species of zebra and is ▶ found only in dry semidesert country of northern Kenya, Ethiopia and Somalia. The numerous fine stripes do not extend onto the belly region, which is always white, and the ears are large and rounded compared with the common Burchell's zebra.

Being primarily a browser, the black rhinoceros ▶▶ thrives in dry thornbush country, although it needs to drink regularly.

In times of drought the elephant can live in country where the black rhinoceros will die of starvation. Not only can it travel greater distances from water but its enormous strength enables it to push over large growing trees, so that it can eat the topmost leaves and twigs. The tusks become tools for survival, stripping off the bark from the main limbs and tree trunk.

The baobab tree provides the elephant with both food and water during times of drought. Using its tusks an elephant can gouge out the moist pith from the bole of a baobab, working as high as fifteen feet or more from the ground.

Very few people have ever seen a baobab tree as ▸ small as this seedling and it is difficult to imagine that it will grow into an obese giant like the one in the background. A baobab grows like a normal tree with a thin trunk until it is about fifteen feet tall: then the trunk starts to swell, and goes on swelling throughout its growing life.

Growing along the river flats, the graceful doum palms are always a welcome sight to a traveller in dry country. Elephants are very fond of the doum nuts, and shake the palms to dislodge the ripe fruit.

Aloes are drought resistant plants, and their bright ▸ flowers add colour to the landscape in thornbush country. The black-headed oriole is mainly a fruit eater, but in this case is feeding from the aloe flowers in the manner of a sunbird, its beak and the front of the head becoming covered with yellow pollen.

The African hare looks very like its European relative and yet it is at home in many hot and dry areas of Africa. It rests in a grassy tussock under a thorn tree during the day, coming out to feed around dusk.

The puff adder is a typical snake of the dry thorn-bush country, living on a variety of rodents and other small mammals. Large puff adders regularly prey on the African hare, and in many areas this is their main diet.

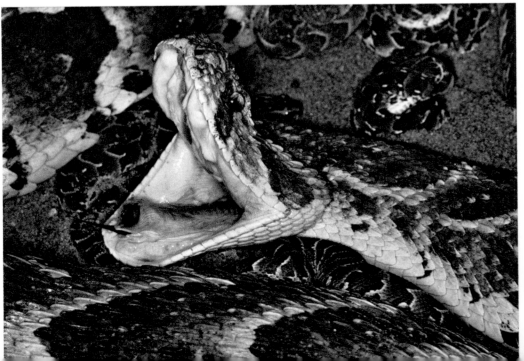

Being strictly nocturnal, the spring hare is seldom seen as it spends the daylight hours in its burrow, emerging at night to hop about searching for its favourite roots and tubers.

The spring hare has developed strong and powerful back legs, and when running hops along like a miniature kangaroo with its long tail held out behind for balance.

Hardly the most handsome of animals, the naked mole rat is rarely seen as it spends its entire life underground, busily digging tunnels as it searches for roots and tubers.

These mounds, like miniature volcanoes, are made by the naked mole rat as it energetically throws loose earth out of its tunnels. The distribution of this strange creature is limited to a small area of northern Kenya and Somalia.

Ground squirrels are a common sight in most dry thornbush areas as they are active during the day, retiring before nightfall to sleep in underground burrows.

Pygmy mongooses are most entertaining creatures to watch as they scurry about in family parties searching for insects, rarely remaining still for long except when basking in the sun.

The dik dik is the smallest antelope found in the dry thornbush country, and even an adult weighs little more than ten or twelve pounds. Note the tiny straight horns of this adult male, above. Dik diks live in pairs, using regular dung heaps in their territory.

◄ Although mainly a grass eater, the hardy beisa oryx will also browse on the leaves of thornbushes, and can exist for long periods without water.

◄◄ Two female gerenuk standing on their hind legs to feed on opposite sides of a bush.

A baby gerenuk has a delicate head and large ears, slender legs and the long neck so characteristic of an adult.

Only the male gerenuks carry horns, and this one must have horns of near-record length. It can easily be seen why the gerenuk is also known as the giraffe-necked gazelle.

Unlike the gerenuk—which never needs to drink water—the impala cannot stray far from permanent water. The overall size and colouration is fairly similar in both these species, but the impala has much larger lyre-shaped horns, even though few males have horns to match this buck, photographed in northern Kenya's Uaso Nyiro Game Reserve.

A yellow-necked francolin or spurfowl rests on the same fallen tree as a dry country sparrow.

Only in close-up can one appreciate the vivid ▶ colouring of a helmeted guinea fowl.

The vulturine is the most handsome species of guinea fowl and is found in the semi-arid areas of Kenya and Somalia.

The caracal, or African lynx, is a feline hunter of ▶ the dry thornbush country: this one is eating a yellow-necked francolin.

The little bushbaby, or galago, is a nocturnal creature, sleeping by day in nests which it makes in well-concealed thickets in the thorn trees, as shown here, or in hollow limbs if these are available.

3 Open Bush and Woodland

The open bush and woodland of central Africa is the vast region, mentioned in the previous chapter, which separates the dry thornbush country of East Africa from a similar area on the west side of southern Africa. It covers southern Tanzania, part of the southern Congo, Malawi, Zambia, Angola, Rhodesia, and also Mozambique except for the coastal plains. In southern Tanzania and in Malawi much of the wooded country is hilly, but in Zambia and Rhodesia it extends for hundreds of miles over fairly flat country. Travel through this uniform vegetation becomes monotonous, mainly because it is impossible to see any distance through the trees or to find a vantage point from which to obtain a view of the surrounding landscape.

Wildlife is fairly plentiful, but game has been killed in some regions by indiscriminate native hunting and by government-sponsored tsetse fly clearing operations. The soil is usually poor and not suitable for the productive farming of cattle or for agriculture; most of the area is therefore sparsely settled. Since wild animals thrive more successfully in this habitat than domestic stock, careful cropping would produce more protein for the human population than ordinary farming.

There are several large animal sanctuaries in this woodland belt, including Zambia's 8,000-square-mile Kafue Game Reserve, which is one of the largest game reserves in Africa. The Luangwa Game Reserve in eastern Zambia is another well-stocked sanctuary, with picturesque riverine vegetation as well as fertile flood plains on either side of the Luangwa River.

The vast Wankie National Park in Rhodesia lies south of the main road that runs between Bulawayo and the famous Victoria Falls. Because of this it attracts more visitors than many of the more remote reserves in similar country. Wankie is an excellent place for studying wildlife typical of this habitat. During the wet season, which lasts for half the year from November until April, much of the game scatters widely, well away from permanent water and the roads used by visitors to the park. However, in the dry winter months the natural catchment areas begin to dry up, and the animals return to where they can find permanent water. Bores have been drilled at strategic points, each fitted with a windmill or pump to keep the waterholes constantly supplied.

Although this woodland country is far more open than a forest, it is surprising how difficult it is to see animals among the trees. A short drive from Main Camp in Wankie, a platform has been built at Nyamandhlovu Pan overlooking the waterhole. Here visitors can sit in comparative comfort while watching the animals as they come to drink. The best period is towards the end of the dry season, from July until late October. Most animals need to drink every day, although not necessarily at the same hour or, for that matter, at the same waterhole. It is therefore possible to see large concentrations of animals at a waterhole on one day, while on the next the same waterhole may remain almost deserted. It is this element of luck which adds suspense to the rewarding pastime of watching game, for one never knows what species of animal, or what exciting incident, will be seen next.

Elephants usually come to drink late in the afternoon, and often herds keep arriving throughout the night. One evening at Wankie, during the dry season, Game Rangers counted the elephants coming to drink at five different waterholes, and there were over 1,500 that night in these places alone. This gives some idea of the concentration of elephants in the Wankie Park during the dry months—many of them are drawn from neighbouring Bechuanaland by the man-made permanent waterholes. It is always interesting to watch elephants drink, as they suck up trunks full of water and then squirt it into their mouths. After drinking twenty gallons or more, an elephant will often have a showerbath, spraying out the water from its trunk. Other elephants may wade out into deeper water to enjoy a plunge bath, bobbing completely under and using the tips of their trunks as snorkels for breathing. An individual animal is often more interesting than the massed scene, and young elephants are always fascinating to watch. A tiny nursing elephant does not drink water, but will enter the waterhole to splash about near the legs of the adults with complete abandon and obvious enjoyment. When a young elephant first attempts to drink water it has a very difficult time as it does not know how to use its trunk. It will kneel to get its mouth right down into the water, often becoming annoyed at the difficulty it has in drinking in this unusual position. When one remembers that an elephant's trunk is actually its elongated nose, it is easy to imagine the problems associated with learning to use it for drinking.

On the whole, elephants do not worry other species of animals around a waterhole, but we did watch one cantankerous old bull which really had a "chip on his shoulder". It was just after noon on an extremely hot day when the lone tusker arrived to drink. He had no sooner waded into the shallow water and begun to drink when he noticed a single warthog trotting down to the waterhole. Turning his attention on the little warthog, the elephant rushed towards it, his trunk swinging viciously from side to side and flaying the water. The warthog halted in amazement, then raced off to safety with its tail held stiffly erect like a flag. After the warthog had disappeared, the elephant waded into deeper water to cool off. Time after time he rolled completely over on his back, with much tossing of his head. Watching this unusual performance we noticed, through binoculars, that his left tusk had been broken off short, and realized that his grumpy behaviour must be due to agonizing toothache. By rolling over in the waterhole he packed the broken tusk with mud which may have relieved the pain, although it was impossible to know if this action was deliberate. While the elephant was still in the water, a beautiful bateleur eagle alighted at the edge of the hole to drink. Again the elephant splashed through the water and was almost on top of the bateleur before it realized the danger and flew off. His quarry having vanished, the elephant stood dejectedly on the bank, his trunk curled up over his head with the tip delicately caressing a ticklish spot behind one ear. Slowly, he began to plod round the edge of the waterhole when three warthogs approached the water. As they were about to pass twenty feet behind the elephant he suddenly wheeled about with an ear-splitting scream, ears spread wide, and swiped at the nearest with his massive trunk. Within seconds the warthogs had vanished and the elephant slowly moved off. A lonely figure without a friend in the world, he soon disappeared in the shimmering heat haze.

Although elephants are the largest land animals living today, they look almost short when seen next to a giraffe. The lofty giraffe cannot simply bend its head down to the water to drink, as its legs are far too long; it must first spread its front legs wide apart, sometimes bending the knees at the same time. Giraffe never seem to attempt to solve this problem by simply wading into the water—probably for fear of getting stuck in the mud.

Giraffe often arrive at a waterhole in small family parties of five or six. As they approach they may be joined by a number of tick birds, which frequently wait in trees near a waterhole, flying down to the arriving animals to search for parasites. Although one giraffe may receive the attentions of a dozen or more tick birds this normally does not worry it unduly. But when it lowers its head to drink the tick birds all hop down its neck and peck away inside its sensitive ears. Time and time again the giraffe will swing upright to vigorously shake the annoying birds off its head. When only one giraffe in a group has its head lowered to drink, tick birds will fly over from the others to congregate on the one animal drinking. It seems that the only way the giraffe can drink in relative peace is when they all have their heads down at the same time—for the tick birds are then spread evenly among the group.

It is around a waterhole that one sees the most interesting combination of animals. A normal buffalo herd in Wankie might number three hundred, but sometimes herds join up so that well over a thousand buffalo come together. We once saw such a herd at Nyamandhlovu Pan. It began drinking at midday and by late afternoon a steady stream was still arriving—the earlier buffalo having moved off to graze well out of sight. When a waterhole is surrounded for so long other animals coming to drink have to mix with the buffalo. During that one afternoon we saw elephant, giraffe, warthog, sable antelope, ostrich, zebra and greater kudu all drinking close to the buffalo. In many years of game viewing we had never seen a sight quite like this. The next day not a single buffalo came to drink at Nyamandhlovu Pan, as the herd had moved on to Dom Pan three miles away.

Sable and greater kudu are two magnificent large antelope which frequent open bush and woodland, and are particularly plentiful in the Wankie National Park. This is undoubtedly the best place in the whole of Africa to see these regal-looking animals, provided one visits the park during the dry winter months. It is arguable whether the sable or the greater kudu bull is the most magnificent antelope. Normally one does not see the two together, though at a Wankie waterhole they will occasionally mix while drinking.

With many large animals about it is easy to overlook some of the smaller visitors. Family groups of warthogs trot smartly down to the water's edge where they kneel to drink. After quenching its thirst, a warthog delights in making a comfortable groove in the mud with its snout and then lies down to enjoy a mudbath. Rolling first on one side, then on the other, it goes through many strange antics as it tries to coat its body thoroughly with a thick layer of cooling mud. If the soil happens to be red a strange-looking animal will emerge, glistening from head to foot with a shiny bright coating. A typical scene of a warthog family having a mudbath, with eland drinking nearby, can be seen on page 126.

There are many animals which, like the warthog, live happily in open woodland as well as on the plains of Africa. Typical of these are the zebra and wildebeest, which are the most common animals on the plains. Of the smaller antelope, the steinbok is found in both habitats, often well away from water, where it may sometimes be seen kicking with a front hoof to uncover succulent grass roots. The larger reedbuck frequents grassy glades in open bush and woodland as well as living in the vicinity of small streams on the plains.

The predators are very much the same in both types of country—lions, leopards, wild dogs and, in areas where they have not been exterminated by man, cheetahs. In the Wankie National Park ratels, or honey badgers, are quite common in some areas, visiting the camps at night in search of scraps of meat. Smaller predators such as caracals, genets, civets and mongooses can also be found, although their distribution may not be continuous. Both the banded and the pygmy mongoose are diurnal, hunting in family parties for insects, lizards, rodents and ground-nesting birds. They are quick and alert little animals, leading a nomadic existence in their continual search for food. Birds of prey are their chief enemies, and a mongoose will sit up straight on its hind legs to search the sky for circling hawks and eagles. When a mongoose utters a shrill, bird-like call, all the others will scurry for safety beneath fallen trees or into holes. Shortly, the little pointed faces peep out from the various hiding places and, if the coast is clear, they resume their search for insects, scratching little holes in the ground wherever they find the faintest scent.

Although ostriches and mongooses are so utterly different, they have one thing in common—both mongooses and ostrich chicks are preyed on by the large martial eagles. The chicks grow up quickly, but when they are very small many are picked up by the big birds of prey. Swooping low, a martial eagle will snatch up an ostrich chick in its talons but, with this extra weight, it cannot regain height quickly. As it flies off just above the ground, the cock ostrich gives chase, striking at it with his powerful feet, and sometimes forcing the eagle to drop its prize. Although bruised and shaken the fortunate little ostrich chick can rejoin its family without any lasting ill effects from its frightening adventure.

As mentioned earlier, wild herds can survive better than domestic stock on the poor woodland soil. For a number of years Mr. John Posselt privately carried out a fine pioneering experiment with the domestication of eland in the Kalahari sand country, in Southern Rhodesia, not far from the borders of both Bechuanaland and South Africa. In this dry area the eland matured much more quickly than cattle and some females gave birth to their first calf just as they reached two years of age. The eland bulls and steers also matured much more quickly than cattle, reaching a weight of 1,500 pounds before they were three years old. Eland are primarily browsers, but will also graze when grass is available. Both sexes are expert at using their horns to break down branches of trees so that they can eat leaves which are otherwise out of reach. The eland unknowingly helps smaller antelope to survive in this dry country, for it moves on without finishing all the leaves.

This is just one small example of how different animals can live in the same environment without competition, and often with direct benefit to each other. Because the different species of wild herbivores in Africa have varied feeding habits, they can live together in greater abundance than domestic stock, without overgrazing and ruining the land. The raising of cattle usually entails cutting down most of the trees to make room for more grass, which often leads to erosion during times of drought and flood. The antelope feed on leaves as well as grass, thereby utilizing the natural vegetation evenly, without destroying the habitat.

This is the attractive main entrance to the Wankie National Park in Rhodesia, an area where mopane trees give cover to a wide variety of game animals. At the end of the dry winter months, around July, August and September, the animals congregate near the permanent waterholes, and this is the best time for game viewing in the Park.

The platform at Nyamandhlovu Pan allows visitors to the Wankie National Park to study game in safety as animals come to drink at the waterhole. Over a thousand individuals made up this herd of buffalo, and they kept arriving throughout the afternoon to slake their thirst, mixing with other animals as they arrived to drink.

An unusual line-up of buffalo horns as all the animals lower their heads to drink side by side. Right: even the solid buffalo cows look small with a stately giraffe standing just behind them at the waterhole.

◄◄ Elephants leave the bush and pass amongst the buffalo on their way to drink peacefully at the water's edge. Although many species of animals concentrate around a waterhole during the dry season they tolerate one another amazingly well, and any type of fight is a rare occurrence—except when a pride of lions take up residence to obtain an easy meal.

The African elephant is the largest land animal living today, but the giraffe is certainly the tallest. It is a rare ►► sight to see the two species close together.

There are many predators in the open bush and woodland, but crocodiles are only found near permanent water. This one is eating a dead wildebeest in the Wankie National Park, and is well known to the Game Rangers who follow its periodic trips between Dom and Nyamandhlovu Pans—a distance of over three miles.

The Cape hunting dog is more frequently seen on the open plains, but also inhabits the vast mopane woodland areas ▸ shown here. They are nomadic, seldom staying more than a few weeks in any one area, and seem to be equally at home in a variety of habitats.
Lions are equally at home on the plains or in the open bush and woodland, but stay clear of thick rain forest or jungle areas.

Long though a giraffe's neck is, it cannot reach down to the surface of the water unless the front legs are first ▸▸ spread wide apart. Although the giraffe appears vulnerable to possible attack in this position, it is ever on the alert and with a quick jerk can resume its normal standing position almost instantly.

Baboons of various species thrive in most habitats of Africa, moving across country on the ground in large troops of between twenty and a hundred, but never venturing far from permanent water. They sleep in trees, or on high rocky kopjes, and like to sit around in the sun in the early morning before moving off in search of food.

The ostrich and the wildebeest below are at home on the plains as well as in open bush. The ostrich family coming to drink is watched by a flock of blacksmith plovers. The long neck and legs hinder an ostrich when drinking—with beak open it scoops at the water several times before raising its head high to allow the water to run down the throat.

Few photographs convey the concentration of animals around a waterhole better than this. Zebras, a favourite prey of lions, are nervous about drinking, and will often spend hours waiting just within the bushes until another species of animal has moved across the open space to drink. The zebras then move down to drink quickly. This had happened in this case, but before the giraffe and the zebras had moved off a herd of elephants also arrived on the scene to drink.

To a photographer an elephant coming towards ▶ the camera, with ears spread wide, looks large and forbidding as it fills the viewfinder.

The real height and bulk of an elephant cannot be ▶▶ fully appreciated until it is seen close to a well-known object such as this Land Rover. Many Game Rangers really love elephants, and Harry Cantle of Wankie is no exception. Studying these massive wild creatures from a distance of only ten feet has given Harry a healthy respect for elephants.

◄ A sable bull walks majestically to the water's edge. Sable antelope inhabit bush country, where they are difficult to photograph away from the water-hole. The Wankie National Park in Rhodesia and the Kruger National Park in South Africa are both good places to see and photograph sable and greater kudu, which are not found in the popular Game Parks of East Africa.

▲ Greater kudu and sable antelope intermingle at a small catchment of water in the Wankie Park.

The greater kudu is undoubtedly the most regal- ▶▶ looking antelope, with long, spiral horns, and it is a wonderful sight to see five big bulls together. Compared to the magnificent males the female at the left looks dainty and insignificant.

Zebras drink while the female kudus timidly approach the water at Dom Pan, where a large crocodile resides (page 112).

A warthog family enjoys a mudbath close to where three eland are drinking. The eland bull in the middle has shorter but more massive horns than the two females.

Eland are the largest of the antelope, but their jumping ability is truly amazing. This eland is easily clearing an eight-foot-wide ditch which is six feet deep. It is well known that impala are the best jumpers among the many smaller antelopes while eland are the champion jumpers of all the larger species.

It has been proved that eland can be domesticated, ▸▸ running well as part of a mixed herd with cattle. While cattle prefer to graze on grasses eland browse on the leaves of trees, and in woodland country this means that almost twice the number of head can be supported without overgrazing.

The domesticated eland mother-to-be likes privacy when giving birth (see the previous page), and will jump over a six-foot fence in order to have her baby in the surrounding bush. Next morning the herdboy has to find the missing antelope and carry the new calf back to the ranch, with the tame mother following on behind.

Elephant break off branches and uproot trees when feeding, but few people know that eland use their horns to break branches when the leaves would otherwise be out of reach. This close-up shows branches broken down by eland, and two eland can be seen in the background to the right.

This big bull eland is in the process of breaking ▶▶ down a branch. The horns are used to hook down a high branch which is then snapped between them, or brought to the front of the head— as in this case—and bent back on itself until broken. Both males and females do this, but seldom stay long enough to eat all the leaves before moving on to new trees. Smaller antelope, such as steinbuck, benefit by this branch-breaking habit of the eland.

Mr. John Posselt has successfully domesticated a herd of eland in Rhodesia, where these photographs were taken. He is weighing Hans, a five-year-old eland ox, finding that its weight of 1,500 pounds hardly varies throughout the year. Eland grow and mature much more quickly than cattle kept under the same conditions, and females often have their first offspring when only two years old.

A number of experiments have been carried out on eland milk, which has more butter fat to the gallon than the richest Jersey cow milk. Dr. Steve Cmelik carried out research with the many interesting fatty acids contained in eland milk when he was in charge of the modern laboratory at Liebig's big Rhodesian canning factory at West Nicholson.

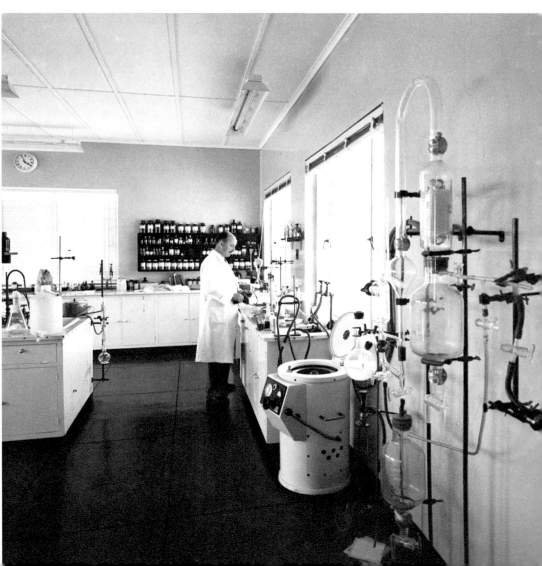

4 The Plains

The best places in the world for watching game today are undoubtedly the great open plains of East Africa. As their average altitude is between three and five thousand feet, the days are pleasantly warm and the nights cool, even though they straddle the equator. By far the largest areas lie south of the equator, stretching through Kenya and the northern half of Tanzania, and to a lesser extent Uganda.

Although the herds on the plains today are only a fraction of those recorded in the past, they are still a most impressive sight. By far the most numerous animals are wildebeest, followed by zebra, with which they associate closely. Other plentiful game are the Thomson's and Grant's gazelles, Coke's hartebeest, topi and, where there are bushes, impala, eland and buffalo. In Uganda, Thomas' kob are common, often associating with topi, and even buffalo. It is interesting that the most common species of Kenya and Tanzania are not found on the grassy flats of western Uganda and the eastern Congo, even though the habitat seems eminently suitable. For instance, in the Queen Elizabeth National Park, Uganda, wildebeest, zebra, Thomson's and Grant's gazelle, impala, eland, Coke's hartebeest, ostrich, giraffe and rhinoceros are absent altogether. In north-western Uganda, the striking Jackson's hartebeest replaces the Coke's hartebeest, and in certain areas giraffe and both black and white rhinoceros are found. Warthogs are common on all the plains of East Africa, and mix freely with other ungulates, or hoofed animals.

Although they are browsers, giraffe spend much time on the plains where there are small acacia trees on which to feed, and do not hesitate to cross completely open areas to reach another belt of trees. In some places giraffe eat the leaves of tiny bushes at ground level, spreading their front feet wide apart, as they do when drinking.

Another animal that is essentially a browser is the black rhinoceros, but many of these animals are found on the open floor of Ngorongoro Crater in Tanzania, where they definitely feed on grass. The much larger white rhinoceros is a grazing animal, and occurs in two widely separated areas. They are plentiful in Zululand, in the north-east of South Africa; they also inhabit north-western Uganda and the neighbouring part of the Sudan. Where both species of rhinoceros occur together, the white rhino eats only grasses while the black rhino feeds on the leaves of bushes.

As the East African plains are so close to the equator there are no summer and winter seasons, but the year divides naturally into the wet and the dry months. There are two wet seasons, known locally as the long and the short rains. The wet months vary slightly in Kenya, Tanzania and Uganda, but the herds breed in each area according to the rains; the baby antelope are born shortly after the new shoots of grass appear.

Wildebeest have definite calving areas, and will migrate a considerable distance each year to reach them. There may not be a single calf in a wildebeest herd on a particular day, while on the next one or two youngsters may be seen, and within a week or ten days every female is likely to be followed by a calf. This very short calving season offers a definite survival advantage. If predators are present—and the spotted hyena usually kills more newly born animals than do lion and leopard combined—the first wildebeests to be born are lucky to survive. However, soon there are hundreds of babies, and the predators cannot eat many in a day, even though the hyenas at this time of year have greatly distended bellies. The young wildebeest grow quickly and within a few weeks are relatively safe. The great majority therefore survive, which would not be the case if the babies were born throughout the year.

Adult wildebeest often band together to chase off a hyena menacing a breeding herd, and many calves are saved by the devoted parents. In the Amboseli Game Reserve we have also seen this happen when a cheetah attacked a baby wildebeest. A herd with young were moving across the plains towards water when they were spotted by a lone cheetah, resting in the open, more than a quarter of a mile away. The cheetah started trotting towards the herd and, on getting close, it raced forward to knock down a young wildebeest in a cloud of dust. The herd ran off and the cheetah lay down to kill the calf by strangulation. Two adult wildebeest then detached themselves from the herd and charged the cheetah, forcing it to run off. The calf then jumped to its feet and was soon back with the herd, not greatly affected by its narrow escape.

There is a place on the Serengeti Plains, where the Seronera River is only a trickle of water connecting a series of secluded pools beneath stately yellow thorn trees, which is especially peaceful and beautiful—far removed from civilization. There are lovely places in other countries, but nowhere else can one find an idyllic setting where nature abounds in such profusion—where perfect peace changes to violence within seconds and returns just as quickly. Nothing could be more peaceful than a herd of delicate-looking Thomson's gazelles grazing in the open, with picturesque yellow thorn trees in the background. The newly born babies are so full of joy that they gambol amongst their elders with a stiff-legged action that is a joy to watch. Tired from the exercise, they pause near their mothers for a quick drink of milk, then lie down in a clump of grass, instinctively flattening their large ears so that they cannot be seen from even a few yards away. Equally peaceful is a nearby scene of two young hyena cubs playing together at the entrance to their underground home, their black baby coats glistening in the sunshine. Not far away their mother is quietly walking amongst the Tommies, large dark eyes ever alert, her shaggy coat constantly ruffled by a cool breeze. Everything is peaceful, and the Tommies take little notice as she passes within yards of where they are quietly grazing. A baby Tommy, flattened and perfectly still, its fawn coat blending with the brownish grass, is passed unnoticed by the hyena. Twenty yards away its playmate of half an hour ago is also hiding, unseen by the hyena. But alas, the second baby loses its nerve and dashes off with the hyena in hot pursuit. The mother gazelle, until this moment apparently unconcerned and taking no notice of the passing hyena, now races ahead of her baby in a series of rapid zigzags, vainly trying to draw off the hyena. But the hyena cannot be sidetracked. In a flurry of dust the drama is over. There is no noise and the end is quick. The other Tommies, which have been watching the chase, resume their grazing. Two jackals appear from apparently nowhere to follow the hyena hopefully. There is peace on the plains once more, and the baby hyenas welcome their mother as she returns from a successful hunt. Being born at this time of the year means that they will not die from starvation.

Although not generally considered carnivorous, there is another animal that preys upon newly born antelope. This is the baboon. Baboons move across the grassy plains eating grass shoots and searching for insects and the eggs of ground-nesting birds. When Thomson's and Grant's gazelles are grazing on the open plains with their newly born young hidden in the grass, a troop of baboons will move amongst the herd, picking up fistfuls of grass to eat as they go along. Also constantly on the lookout for baby gazelles hiding in the grass, the big baboons catch a surprising number during the week or two when they are being born.

The most remarkable of all the incidents we have filmed concerning baboons and baby antelope occurred in the Serengeti just after midday on the 17th January, 1958. A big male baboon was sitting in the open, busily starting to eat a baby Grant's gazelle it had just killed. Suddenly it was chased by an irate female Grant's gazelle, which pursued it across a stretch of open ground until the baboon found sanctuary in a large yellow thorn tree. Cautiously the baboon would descend the tree, only to be forced up again by the female gazelle. Time passed, and the mother Grant started to graze away from the tree. Not needing a second opportunity, the baboon was down the tree like a flash, looking back over his shoulder as he raced towards another tree. As he climbed to safety, the sharp horns of the charging female Grant's gazelle only missed him by inches. The conflict went on for three hours, with the baboon no sooner descending one tree than he had to race for the safety of yet another. This personal battle raged back and forth between three trees in the open and, in the meantime, the rest of the baboon troop moved out of sight. What would be the outcome of all this? The baboon was definitely frightened of the female Grant, and yet it was obvious that the gazelle did not want to risk a fight with the powerful male baboon. She worried and tormented him without actually drawing blood. The end came suddenly and unexpectedly! The battle brought the female Grant back to the place where her dead baby had been dropped in the grass by the baboon, and she looked at it without moving for perhaps half a minute. When the bereaved mother realized that the baby was dead, and therefore past her help, she walked off slowly towards the herd without a backward glance at the baboon, which was now racing off in the opposite direction. It had been a very touching and moving scene and it was hard to believe that a female antelope would remember and hold a grudge against another animal for so long—yet the colour film fully records the whole encounter.

The Serengeti is undoubtedly the best place in Africa for seeing leopards, which are shy, nocturnal creatures seldom found in action during daylight. In a forest, leopards can never be seen hunting, but on the plains they can be followed at a distance without being disturbed. Surely no one can fail to be awed by the sinuous grace of a leopard walking through an open glade, with sunlight laying a sheen on its spotted coat.

Near Seronera we have filmed leopards in thorn trees with various kills, such as a young topi antelope and even a young zebra. However, the most thrilling sight of all was when we filmed one taking a full-grown male Thomson's gazelle high into a yellow thorn tree. The leopard paused on the ground with the Tommy lying between its legs, looking up into the tree to judge the distance to the lowest branch, before taking a firm grip on the kill with its jaws. Then, from a point at least three feet from the base of the tree, it made a tremendous leap to grip the trunk with its strong claws. With every sinew straining it clawed its way up into the tree, until the carcass could be deposited in the lowest fork. Pausing for breath, the leopard looked up into the higher branches before picking up the prize again and dragging it to a higher branch, where it balanced the carcass so that it would not fall to the ground. With the larder stocked and safe from hyenas, the leopard stretched out along a branch to rest.

The Serengeti is famous for its lions, and rightly so. Here the King of Beasts has found a natural paradise. For a lion paradise means plenty of game, open country over which to gaze, shady trees whenever needed, permanent water, and freedom from biting flies. To this, one must add protection from the only ruthless killer in the animal kingdom—man!

Lions are so strong and powerful, and so skilled at stalking, that one is inclined to think they have no trouble in making a kill. But this is far from the truth. How many times have we watched lions stalking, and approach so close to their intended victims that it seemed they could not possibly miss—only to find that at the last minute the quarry moved off as if by instinct, or perhaps warned by scent carried to them by a slight change in wind direction. When hunting, lions are frustrated more often than they are rewarded with success. They are basically lazy animals, and after a large meal are very happy to rest in the shade of trees for a few days before worrying about the next meal. Lions do not kill for the sake of killing, but only when they are hungry.

The family plays an important part in the life of a lion, and cubs can play with any lioness or even with the big male in a pride. If more than one lioness has young cubs it is not unusual to see a cub nurse from one before getting up and suckling from a second, and this passes without fuss on the part of the mothers. It is quite common for a number of lionesses with cubs to band together, and often one lioness will baby-sit while the others go hunting. A lone lioness with tiny cubs is likely to lose them to a hungry hyena whenever she has to leave them while hunting.

A pride of lions often use teamwork when stalking game. By circling behind a herd of grazing animals one lion can stampede them towards the other lions which are spread out in concealment. Once a kill has been made, all members of the pride share in the meal—the baby-sitting lioness bringing up the cubs for their share. Family life is not quite idyllic, as the stronger lions make sure they get the choicest meat, while the cubs have to look after themselves. But with a zebra or wildebeest kill there is plenty for each member of the pride, and enough left over for the scavengers.

The scavengers of the plains play a very important role in preventing the spread of disease. Hyenas and jackals have an excellent sense of smell and effectively clean up the remains of a lion's kill; hyenas can crack all but the largest bones, and these are often gnawed by porcupines. Vultures are active during daylight, and with their keen sight they miss nothing on the plains as they circle overhead. When one vulture sights a kill and spirals down, it is seen by others, which fly in from miles around to join the feast. There is little left when they have finished, but ants are always present to take away the tiniest scraps. It is surprising how even large animal carcasses can disappear almost without trace, so efficient is the work of nature's sanitation corps. There is no wastage in nature, as the chemical components of all plants and animals return to the soil, ready to fertilize new plant growth—which in turn will support new animal life.

Seen from the air, game trails are often so well defined that they resemble highways, with a spidery web of secondary tracks branching from the main thoroughfare.

It is almost impossible to show, in one interesting photograph, the full story of the open plains, with vast numbers of game spread out across the grassland. The grazing animals dot the plains, often with the different species mixing freely, as shown by these zebras and Grant's gazelles. The thin line of thornbushes in the background is also typical, indicating where a stream flows during the rainy season.

This immature male Grant's gazelle is a handsome creature, even though ▶▶ it does not have fully developed horns.

At this early age it is not easy to tell the difference between a Grant's ▶▶▶ and a Thomson's gazelle from its face. They are both equally appealing, but this is a young Tommy, as a Thomson's gazelle is affectionately called in East Africa.

These Thomson's gazelles are considerably smaller than Grant's gazelles, and are a much brighter orange-buff colour with a very clearly defined black stripe along each side of the body. A Tommy's tail is black, and the white on the rump does not extend above the base of the tail as it does with a Grant. Both sexes carry horns, but those of the female are short and quite slender, as can be seen in this photograph taken on the Serengeti Plains, Tanzania. Thomson's gazelles are very alert little antelope, whose black tails are constantly flicking back and forth. In fact, there is a saying that the only time a Tommy stops wagging its tail is when it is dead.

The ringed horns of this adult male Tommy are very well developed, and seldom grow longer. This open setting is in the Masai Amboseli Game Reserve, Kenya.

Zebra in a park-like setting beneath spectacular
yellow acacias, or thorntrees, near the Seronera
River in the vast Serengeti Plains.

The size of an ostrich, the largest living bird, can be appreciated when compared with these adult zebra and wildebeest. The striking black and white plumage of the male is in marked contrast to the dull brownish colouration of the female.

The mottled colouring of an ostrich chick does ▶ not resemble either of its parents. To see this pert little creature it is hard to realize the struggle it had to break out of the egg unaided, as shown in detail on the following pages.

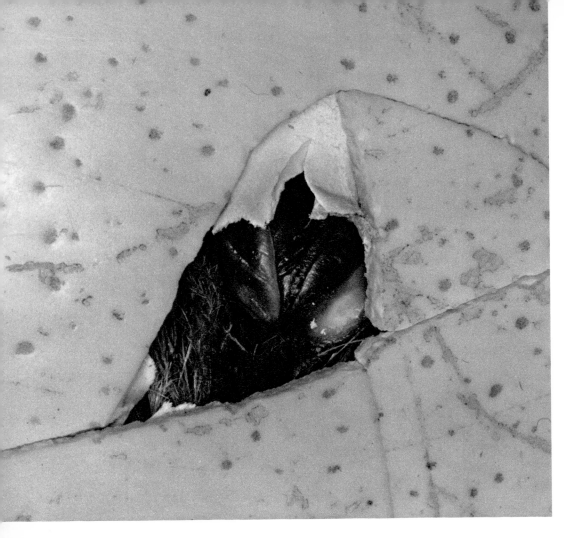

The first stage of its epic struggle is over—the little ostrich chick has succeeded in making the initial opening in the thick shell. Worn out by this exertion it rested for several hours, calling in a characteristic trill from time to time—a sound so loud that it was hard to believe that it came from a chick still imprisoned within the egg.

After a long rest the chick resumes its struggle, pushing outwards with the egg tooth on the tip of its beak, and turning over within the egg.

The egg itself has not moved, but the progress of the chick turning within the egg can be clearly seen. Not only must the thick shell be broken into small pieces along the line of rotation, but the thick and leathery inner skin also has to be torn.

With head and neck folded under its body, and legs folded at the sides, the chick heaves, pushing the two sections ▸▸ of the shell apart. The wiry nature of its baby feathers can be clearly seen.

▲ After many exhausting hours of work the chick is at last free of the shell, and momentarily worn out. Soon it will stagger clumsily to its feet, and begin pecking at pieces of grass and small stones. The big adventure of life in the outside world has begun.

The pretty little bat-eared fox lives in burrows on ▶ the open plains, and feeds mainly on grasshoppers and other insects. Although they do most of their feeding at night, bat-eared foxes are often to be seen sunning themselves at the entrance to their burrow during the day.

A black rhinoceros sleeping right out in the open ▶▶ on the dusty plains in the Masai Amboseli Game Reserve. A spurt of dust flies each time the sleeping rhino exhales.

◄ It is usual to think of monkeys inhabiting the thick rain forests or jungles of Africa, and that is certainly where many species are to be found. However, the vervet monkey has a very wide distribution, with numerous local races found all the way from West Africa through central to eastern and southern Africa. Vervets inhabit forests too, but are even more at home in open country. Baby vervets are cute little things with black fur and pink faces; later these change to the adult colouration of grey fur and a black face.

A picturesque tree growing on the rim of Ngorongoro Crater in Tanzania, with rain falling on the far side of the crater ten miles away. Long extinct, Ngorongoro is the largest volcanic crater in the world and is surrounded by walls 1,000 feet or more high. The crater floor is mainly open grassland with plentiful water and, together with the adjoining Serengeti Plains, forms one of the finest areas in Africa for plains game.

Leopards frequently snarl when approached in the ►► open in daylight.

In open country leopards usually spend the daylight hours near streams where there are trees. This leopard has taken its kill, a young topi antelope, into a tree to keep it away from hyenas. The leopard's spotted coat affords it excellent camouflage when lying in dappled sunlight filtered through the leaves of a tree. Being mainly nocturnal, as well as naturally shy and secretive, the graceful leopard is not often seen in action even in areas where it is quite common.

Having non-retractile claws cheetahs are not considered to be tree climbers, but they like to take advantage of any high place to view the surrounding countryside.

A large fallen tree provides a fine vantage point for cheetahs to view the distant scene. They have excellent eyesight, and can spot a prospective meal at a considerable distance, long before the quarry is aware that there are predators in the vicinity.

◄◄ A close-up of a cheetah snarling, with a fly perched on its nose, and showing the characteristic black "teardrop" marking under the eye. This also shows very clearly the dentition of a full grown cheetah, with teeth well adapted for gripping and cutting through sinewy meat.

Topi antelope are animals of the plains, occurring in the Serengeti, but in even greater numbers in the Kigezi section of Uganda's Queen Elizabeth National Park, where this picture was taken. Here herds of up to two thousand animals have been counted on the one open plain, mixing freely with Thomas' kob as well as herds of buffalo.

Thomas' kob, called the Uganda kob in East Africa, is a larger and stockier antelope than the better-known impala, but in both species only the males have horns.

This long shot of a herd of buffalo, accompanied by a flock of cattle egrets, clearly shows the type of country in the Kigezi area of Uganda's Queen Elizabeth National Park, which borders the Congo.

A new growth of grass adds colour to the park-like setting for these buffalo, photographed in the Murchison Falls National Park, in north-western Uganda, close to the border of both the Congo and the Sudan. A scene like this is only possible when fires have burnt off the six-foot-high elephant grass, and recent rain has brought on new green shoots of grass. Within a month the grass is likely to be high enough partly to hide the buffalo from view.

A male Coke's hartebeest or kongoni is one of the larger plains antelope, and is regarded by many people as a stupid-looking animal with its sloping hindquarters and long pointed face. Both sexes carry horns of approximately equal size, which stick out from the head at a similar angle to the ears, creating a strange "four horned" effect.

Two female Coke's hartebeest with young, in the Nairobi National Park.

Wildebeest follow the leader along a game trail across the open plains.

A mother and baby brindled gnu, or white- ▶▶ bearded wildebeest.

An old bull elephant, with unusual crossed tusks, ▶▶▶ in the Queen Elizabeth Park.

The secretary bird is a very distinctive bird of the plains, as it strides about on the ground in search of insects, small mammals, lizards and snakes. It is also a threat to the chicks of ground nesting birds such as the crowned plover, shown on page 182. With its large wings the secretary bird is an excellent flier, but prefers to remain almost continually on the ground unless disturbed. These birds have the hooked beak typical of birds of prey, and obtain their name from the long black quill-like feathers at the back of the head. Their large stick nests are made on top of very thick thorn trees, sometimes no more than ten feet from the ground, but usually very well hidden.

Ground hornbills are comical-looking birds usually seen in small groups of about three to six, strutting about on the ground searching for insects, reptiles and small mammals. An idea of the bird's large size is given by the presence of the male kob. In close-up the large beak can be clearly seen, as well as the extremely long eye-lashes.

A crowned plover shades her speckled eggs from ▶▶ the heat of the noonday sun, which is vertically overhead, near the equator. The nest is simply a shallow depression in the soil, usually right out in the open on the treeless plain.

The adult warthog has large wart-like protuberances on the sides of its face. Bristly hairs sparsely cover the greyish skin, with a mane of long black hairs along the neck and back. Warthogs live in family groups, and it is a most amusing sight to see the whole family running off in line astern, all with tails held stiffly erect. This group is watched by three female kob in the Murchison Falls National Park, Uganda.

▲ A lion cub playing with a stone is as charming as any baby animal can be, but even at this early age its paws are already huge.

A lioness yawns, showing off her fangs and long rough tongue. ▶

▼ There seems to be a deadly purpose behind the long strides of this black-maned lion. In fact, a lioness has made a kill a quarter of a mile away and the "king" is not wasting any time before claiming his share of the meal.

◀◀◀ The "king of beasts" spends much of the day resting under a shady tree. This is a large yellow-maned lion of the Serengeti, an area famous for its fine lions.

◀◀ A young male lion demonstrates his tremendous strength as he pulls a waterbuck carcass into the shade of a tree.

▲ After lions have left the scene of a kill a spotted hyena takes over, dragging away large bones which it is able to crack in its powerful jaws.

A vulture waits patiently in a nearby tree, ready ▶ to fly down to the ground as soon as the lions leave the kill.

Magnificent flyers and graceful soarers on the thermals, a vulture glides down to clean up the open plains after lions have moved away from their kill. Vultures have been aptly named "nature's sanitation corps", leaving no meat to rot and spread disease. To some people they are repulsive, but they play an important role in the pattern of nature's paradise.

5 The Changing Scene

The vegetation in any area changes in a regular yearly cycle. In much of Africa there is no real winter, but the wet and the dry seasons alter the appearance of the countryside. During the dry season the trees lose their leaves, and grass dries up as it does in winter on other continents. The wet season produces rapid new growth, and resembles spring and summer. These weather changes affect animal life just as much as vegetation. During the rains there is plenty of green grass, and the trees put out new leaves and flowers, while most animals have their young.

On occasions, however, much greater local changes take place. Some of these are due to natural causes such as drought, flood or fire, but in other cases it is man that upsets the balance of nature. All too frequently overgrazing by cattle, sheep and goats, together with poor farming methods, opens the way for erosion. When the rains break after a severe drought there is usually flooding, for the water cannot soak into the hard and parched earth, and the run-off carries away much of the rich topsoil, thus depleting the land still further.

Sometimes floods are made by man. When the 420-foot-high Kariba Dam was built across the Zambezi River it created one of the largest artificial lakes in the world, nearly two hundred miles long and up to forty miles wide. This man-made lake is in rich game country, where elephant, black rhinoceros, lion, leopard, buffalo, sable antelope, greater kudu, impala, bushbuck, water-buck, duiker, steinbok, grysbok, klipspringer, warthog, bush pig, civet, genet, aardvark, pangolin, baboon, vervet monkey, bushbaby and tortoise were all living in peace along the banks of the mighty river. After the dam was completed it took several years for the lake to fill up completely. Each year, as the water rose, the new lake flooded side valleys, creating islands of the high ground. Many animals were trapped on these islands which, as the floodwaters continued to rise, diminished in size until eventually most were inundated. The marooned animals soon stripped the shrinking islands of all available food. Only the carnivores found life easy.

Fortunately man, who had created the problem, helped to solve it. Most of the rescue work at Kariba was done by the "Operation Noah" team of the Wild Life Conservation Department of Southern Rhodesia. Other funds were provided by the Fauna Preservation Society of Britain and administered by Northern Rhodesia, now Zambia. Rupert Fothergill led the "Operation Noah" rescue team, which consisted of a handful of Europeans and about forty African helpers. No rescue operation of this type had previously been attempted, so the team had new problems to solve almost daily.

Of all the animals on the islands the elephant proved to be the most sensible, recognizing the danger and swimming to the mainland before the habitat was completely destroyed. Usually they swam off during the night, but occasionally a rescue team would find two or three elephants right out in the open water of the lake. If the boat came too close, the elephants panicked and nearly drowned in their terrified haste to get away. So the men learnt to stay well back, whilst ensuring that the elephants swam in the right direction to reach the mainland at the closest point.

A strange fact learnt at Kariba was that lions had absolutely no fear of the water. They swam regularly between the islands, where they found hunting conditions ideal. One pride of six lions swam three miles from the mainland to reach Long Island in the middle of Lake Kariba. As the floodwaters rose this island split into three smaller islands. Before the lions were captured they used to swim regularly between these islands which were then several hundred yards apart.

Strong rope nets proved the most effective method for catching the antelope and warthogs. A ten-foot-high net was hung between trees across the narrowest part of an island. Then the men would beat the bushes and make a lot of noise as they gradually worked their way towards the concealed net. As soon as an animal ran into the net the men would catch it and tie it up with soft ropes made from plaited nylon stockings. Because of their formidable tusks, warthogs had to have their jaws as well as their legs securely tied. The captured animals were tagged for future reference, and then placed in fast boats for the trip to the mainland where they were released.

Catching and moving the rhinos proved a big job, but it was handled efficiently. These heavy-weights had first to be immobilized. This was done by darting each rhino with a drug-filled hypodermic fired from a special capture gun. The correct dosage of the drug had to be administered to anaesthetize the rhino, and while this was taking effect the animal was followed closely so that an antidote could be given as soon as it became immobilized. While the rhino was unconscious, the men would quickly tie its legs together with strong ropes. When the dangerous and exciting part of the work had been completed, the really hard work began. An adult black rhinoceros weighs about one and a half tons, and the anaesthetized beast might well be several hundred yards from the water. Some men would at once begin to clear a track through the bush to the lake, while others laboured to roll the rhino on to a wooden platform, which was fitted with two skids. When the animal was safely secured on the sledge, the men pulled this along the track to the water's edge, at which point the rhino had to be moved on to a barge for its trip to the mainland. When released, many an ungrateful rhinoceros charged its rescuers before running off into the bush. This was not the introduction of a new species, as the black rhinoceros lived in the Wankie area many years ago.

Before "Operation Noah" came to a successful conclusion at the end of 1962, a new wildlife crisis developed. In July of that year a large colony of approximately two million flamingoes started to nest at Lake Magadi, seventy miles south-west of Nairobi. Flamingoes live on a chain of barren soda lakes dotting the Great Rift Valley in eastern Africa. It is an inhospitable place. Searing winds blow almost continuously and during the day the temperature soars to 120°F. Subterranean thermal springs feed Lake Magadi with a supply of alkaline water and, as the lake has no outlet, it forms a large evaporating pan some eighteen miles long and two miles wide. Because there is no drainage the soda becomes concentrated and forms a surface crust which in some places is ten to twelve feet thick.

In previous years the flamingoes had nested on huge Lake Natron, thirty miles to the south of Lake Magadi, in a spot where they could not be approached by man because of the treacherous nature of the soda crust. In 1962 heavy rains flooded the Lake Natron nesting grounds, causing the flamingoes to move to Lake Magadi. This was the first time that lesser flamingoes had nested in an accessible spot where they could be studied in detail. Towards the end of August the chicks began hatching in countless thousands. When the young birds were ten or twelve days old they left the nests, and banded together in large groups near the centre of the vast nesting area. Evaporation had now changed the shallow lake into a death trap, for the soda crystallized on their legs and eventually formed heavy anklets which impeded movement. Weakened by this weight the chicks floundered in the brine. Many struggled, fell and finally became so weak that they were unable to move. The merciless sun beat down on the desolate expanse of Lake Magadi, and the chicks died, their bodies caked in the soda crust.

Alan and Joan Root, who had been filming the nesting birds, hurried to Nairobi to sound the alarm. The story of the flamingoes' plight was quickly spread around the world by the press, the radio and television. Almost overnight, the appeal fund was over-subscribed. Many people, including army and air force units, and school children from Magadi, helped with the rescue work. The men manually freed 27,000 chicks by cracking the solid anklets off the young flamingoes' legs. Then rain fell at Magadi and as the water in the lake rose the soda content was considerably reduced, with the result that the anklets on the remaining chicks dissolved. It is estimated that 400,000 young flamingoes survived.

As the chicks matured many were caught and banded by members of the East African Natural History Society. This was the first time that both lesser and greater flamingoes had been banded in quantity, and it is hoped that the operation will throw new light on the periodic movements of these interesting and beautiful birds.

Capturing dangerous big game animals is exciting and strenuous work. At Ngamo Pan, in a remote section of the vast Wankie National Park in Rhodesia, surplus animals are caught to stock new National Parks in other regions of the country. Animals such as giraffe, buffalo, sable antelope, greater kudu, wildebeest, roan antelope, impala and eland were once plentiful throughout most of Rhodesia, but with the spread of civilization they can no longer be seen near the main cities so two relatively small areas—the McIlwaine National Park near Salisbury, and the Matopos National Park near Bulawayo—have been stocked in recent years with a variety of big game species. In these small parks the animals live a natural life where they once roamed in great numbers.

The Game Rangers of Wankie have worked out an ingenious method of capturing and moving giraffe and other animals. They operate during the dry winter months when the animals come to drink at Ngamo Pan, which is surrounded by an area of open country flanked on all sides with woodland. The animals can be seen as they leave the bush and move out across the plain on their way to drink. Two stripped-down Land Rovers are used to chase them across the sandy clearing; maximum speed is essential in order to overtake the fleeing herd before it reaches the safety of the trees, where it is impossible for vehicles to follow. As an animal is overtaken a noose is deftly slipped over a rear hoof and pulled tight. After capture animals such as eland, sable, roan, wildebeest, kudu and young buffalo are immediately lifted into the back of a Land Rover and driven direct to the holding pens. Two Land Rovers are used because it is intended that two animals from the same herd should be caught, for this will result in them settling down immediately when placed in the pen.

At Ngamo Pan the animals come to drink in the open close to where the holding pens have been constructed in advance (an unusual feature of game capturing). After capture only minutes elapse before the animals are released into a holding pen. The other thing that is unusual about the Ngamo Pan captures is the type of harness devised for giraffe. After a giraffe has been caught by a hind leg, a long stick is used to place a blanket over its head. Once blindfolded the animal stands still and allows a special harness to be buckled around its body. To this, three ropes are attached—one in front and one on either side. When the blanket is removed the giraffe bounds forward, and the men holding the long guide ropes also run forward; in this way the giraffe is guided to the holding pens without having to be manhandled. As a result, the whole capture operation often takes less than half an hour.

Usually, within a week the required number of animals have been assembled in the pens. Then they are loaded on to trucks and driven several hundred miles to their new homes. On arrival they walk straight out of the crates into natural bush country. The McIlwaine National Park near Salisbury, and the Matopos National Park near Bulawayo, have both been stocked with animals caught at Ngamo Pan in Wankie. The captured animals settle down at once and form the nucleus of breeding herds. Since both parks are close to the big cities, the animals can be watched and appreciated by people who would never be able to visit the Wankie National Park.

A totally different type of game-capture operation took place in Kenya during the latter half of 1963. The Hunter's antelope, which is also called the Hunter's hartebeest *(Damaliscus hunteri)*, is a little-known and almost forgotten animal. It has never been exhibited in any zoo, and few people have seen it in the wild state for it lives in a very restricted plains area inland from the coast on the border of Kenya and Somalia, between the Tana and Juba rivers. The Hunter's antelope is found nowhere else in the world.

In November 1962, it was announced that the United Nations Special Fund would finance a £500,000 survey in the lower Tana River area for land suitable for irrigation and intensive human settlement. This alarmed international conservation circles, as no provision had been made for the Hunter's antelope should its habitat be used for intensive farming. The Kenya Game Department immediately started a biological survey of the area, as well as checking for similar habitats elsewhere in the country. It was decided to capture the nucleus of a breeding herd of Hunter's antelope and move them one hundred and sixty miles to the Tsavo National Park. The animals were easily caught, but many did not survive the bumpy, round-about road journey to their new home in Tsavo.

When the Royal Navy's aircraft carrier "Ark Royal" arrived in Mombasa the idea of "Operation Antelope" was born, and many people cooperated to bring about its success. The delicate Hunter's antelope were flown by helicopter direct from the base camp at Buna, on the Tana River, to the Tsavo release point. All twenty animals arrived in perfect condition after the one-hour flight, bringing to thirty the number of Hunter's antelope released in the Tsavo National Park.

The natural scene is changing rapidly throughout the world, but perhaps nowhere faster than in Africa. Fortunately international conservation societies are helping the dedicated men working in the field. Many small gifts from individual people throughout the world confirm the fact that we humans do care about the plight of wildlife, and hope to ensure its survival for future generations to enjoy.

Erosion can become a serious problem in any country where overgrazing and drought drastically reduce the vegetation cover. Heavy downpours of rain, with rapid run-off of water, then carry the rich topsoil away. ▶

Only from the air can the insidious fingers of erosion be seen properly, all leading into the dry river beds. ▶▶

When a long drought strikes many cattle starve to death. Emaciated carcasses of dead beasts are piled in heaps, dried out like parchment in the hot, air. For once the scavengers are unable to cope. ▶▶▶

◀ As surely as day follows night, so must rain follow drought. In this scene of flooding in north-eastern Kenya the course of streams can be followed by the twin line of trees dotting their former banks.

Man-made flooding: the building of the 420-foot-high Kariba Dam in Rhodesia, completed in 1960, transformed a 200-mile stretch of the Zambesi Valley into one of the largest man-made lakes in the world.

The Zambesi Valley is rich game country, and flooding concentrated the wildlife on newly formed islands—which were in turn flooded as the new lake rose higher and higher. Here men of the "Operation Noah" game rescue team reverse a boat to save a female duiker antelope.

A grysbok attempts to hide in the partly submerged foliage, but is soon spotted and picked up by one of the "Operation Noah" rescue teams.

On being lifted into the boat the animals' legs are tied together with plaited nylon stockings, which do not chafe as a rope would. Small, fast boats then take the captured animals several miles to the nearest point on the mainland for release. Here a helper carries a female duiker ashore to be released.

On the mainland a male impala bounds away as soon as the nylon stockings are removed.

More people in the "Operation Noah" team were injured by warthogs than by any other species of animal, including large animals such as sable, kudu, waterbuck, lions, rhinos and buffaloes. The warthog's vicious tusks can only be safely controlled by placing a noose over both jaws and pulling it tight. Great care had to be taken when releasing warthogs, as they were likely to charge their rescuers. This warthog is about to be released in shallow water from the safety of a boat—he will be free as soon as the tension on the noose is slackened, and he will then wade ashore through the shallow water.

It was a great personal triumph for Rupert Fothergill, who was in charge of "Operation Noah", when he successfully caught this lioness in a box trap. She was released on the mainland, but had to swim the last few yards to shore so that she would not turn on her rescuers in the boats.

While "Operation Noah" was still in progress in 1962 a new wildlife problem was developing at Lake Magadi, far away in Kenya. This oily-looking film is actually a drying crust of soda. Lake Magadi has no outlet, but is fed by alkaline water from underground springs. Evaporation concentrates this saline water, eventually forming a surface crust of dry soda crystals.

During the latter half of 1962 an estimated one million pairs of flamingoes nested on Lake Magadi, only 70 miles from Nairobi. All went well until most of the chicks left the nests, then disaster struck—the shallow water through which the chicks continually waded had an extraordinarily high soda content, causing the death of many young.

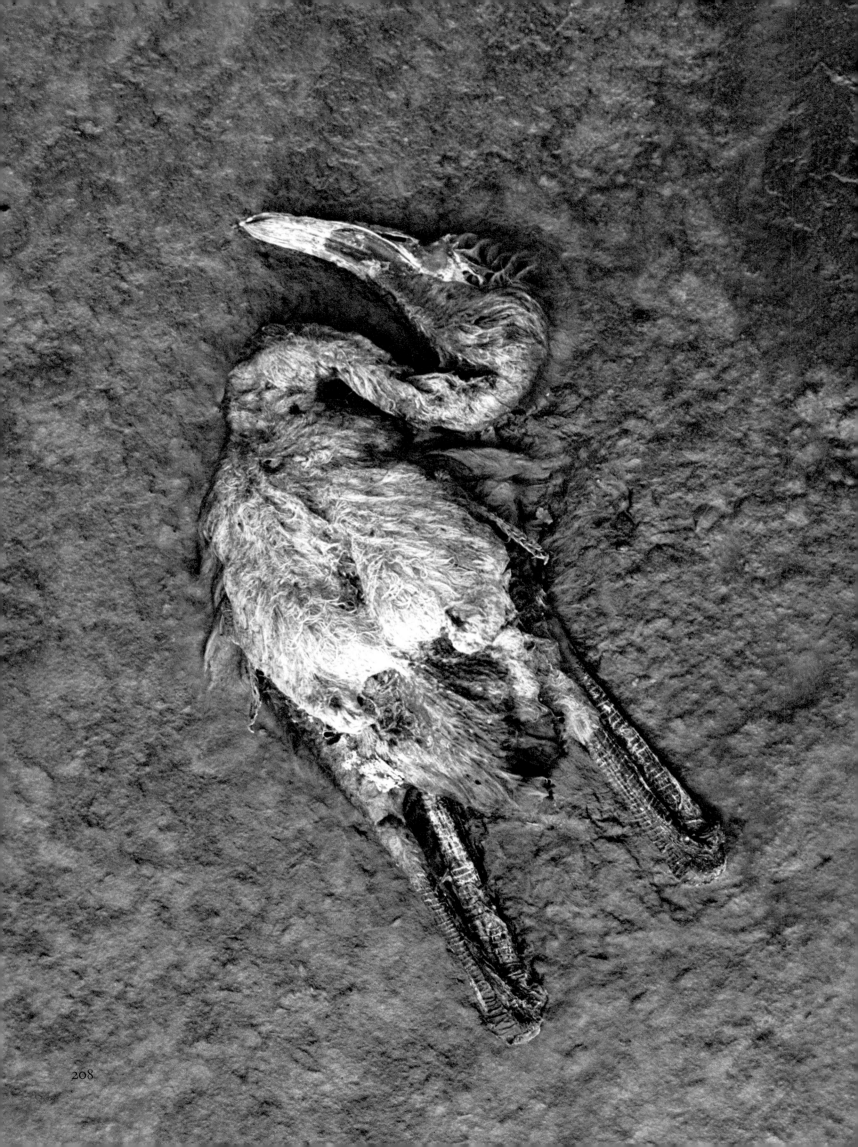

Members of the East African Natural History Society herded a number of young flamingoes into pens, to be banded and released, in order to learn more about the yearly movements of these mysterious birds for the future.

With many eager hands at work the flamingo chicks are soon caught, and handed over the fence to the men doing the banding. Alan Root (left), banding one of the chicks, organized the rescue operation at Lake Magadi, working for many weeks to remove the anklets of rock-hard soda crystals which had formed on the legs of the chicks.

Above, a newly banded chick races off across the hard soda crust to join the other young flamingoes. Altogether an estimated 400,000 chicks survived the "Ordeal of the Soda" at Lake Magadi during the 1962 nesting season.

Natural relief came with the breaking of the rains, reducing the soda concentration of the lake water and dissolving the anklets on the remaining chicks.

Game Rangers of the vast Wankie National Park in Rhodesia visit Ngamo Pan towards the end of the dry season for the purpose of capturing a number of animals needed to stock newly formed National Parks near the main cities of Salisbury, Bulawayo and Livingstone. Here the men are carrying out the difficult and dangerous task of capturing an immature buffalo from amongst a large herd which had come out into the open to drink, 60 miles from Main Camp.

211

A giraffe races across the plain, all four feet off the ground at the same time.

As the capture vehicle draws near to the galloping giraffe the men are ready with a short pole fitted with a rope noose at the end. The noose is slipped over the animal's nearside rear hoof when this is momentarily off the ground, and the giraffe is gradually brought to a halt.

A long pole is used to place a blanket over the animal's head as a blindfold, and with this in place the giraffe soon settles down. A specially made harness is buckled onto the body, and three guide ropes are attached to this harness.

When the guide ropes are attached to the body harness the giraffe walks and runs towards the previously prepared holding pen, with the men steering it in the right direction.

A giraffe seems to be a naturally tame animal, and ▸ is soon looking placidly out of the pen at the human activity going on around the camp. It takes three giraffe to make a truckload, but these are soon caught by the efficient capture team.

A blanket is used over the giraffe's head once more when it is caught in the pen, and the guide ropes ensure that it leaves the enclosure and enters the truck safely. On the long journey by road telephone wires have to be lifted to allow the giraffe truck to pass underneath. On arrival at their new home one giraffe looks out from the back of the truck before being released.

In Rhodesia giraffe, buffalo, sable, roan, wildebeest, kudu and impala were caught in order to stock new National Parks closer to the big cities, where the animals had been plentiful before the coming of civilization. All the animals moved were ones which were not threatened with extinction. But it was a very different story in Kenya with the capture of the rare Hunter's antelope, which are found only in a very small area north of the Tana River in north-eastern Kenya and also in part of southern Somalia. No one knows definitely just how many Hunter's antelope there are, but the highest reliable estimate is around 1,000 animals. There are none in any of the world's zoos, and so if anything happened to the Hunter's antelope in this one small area it would mean the extinction of the species. It was therefore decided to try to establish a small herd of these animals in a second area, several hundred miles away, in the Tsavo National Park. The capture team of the East African Wild Life Society combined with the Kenya Game Department to carry out this difficult task. The plan became known as "Operation Antelope".

Once a Hunter's antelope is roped it has to be quietened down. Tony MacGuire, in charge of the Wild Life Society's capture team, nearly falls as he struggles with a new captive; but it soon settles down and stands quietly.

By first blindfolding the Hunter's antelope it could be safely lifted into the vehicle without a struggle. With three men holding it in the back of the truck Tony MacGuire drives back to camp to release the animal in the holding enclosure.

The Hunter's antelope settled down in enclosures for several days, and were then caught and placed in individual crates for the journey to their new home in Tsavo National Park, an eighteen-hour drive by road but only a one-hour journey by helicopter.

The Royal Navy aircraft carrier "Ark Royal" visited Mombasa, and its helicopters assisted with "Operation Antelope"—an unusual training exercise for the crews amid dust, more than 100 miles from the sea.

After their journey by helicopter the Hunter's antelope rested quietly in pens for several days before the gates were opened and the animals allowed to wander slowly off into their new home in the Tsavo National Park. It is hoped that the thirty animals released in Tsavo will settle down and breed, thus establishing the species in a second, more accessible area.

6 The Lakes

Many countries have only fresh-water lakes, but in Africa there are alkaline lakes as well. The lakes of Africa therefore provide two different types of habitat. Some species of birds are found in both environments, but the majority of the fauna show a definite preference for either one or the other. Fish life in the fresher lakes is particularly prolific, and many of the lakes have numerous endemic species of mouth-breeders. Where fish are plentiful it is usual to find rich bird life, and this is certainly true of the wonderful lakes of eastern Africa.

Many of the large lakes in this region are in the Great Rift Valley, which stretches from the Jordan Valley and the Red Sea south through eastern Africa to Mozambique. In East Africa the Rift Valley forks, the eastern arm running from Ethiopia southward through Kenya and Tanzania; the western branch approximately along the boundary between Uganda and the Congo. The forks of the Rift Valley join in the south close to where the boundaries of Tanzania, Zambia and Malawi meet. Lake Tanganyika, in the Western Rift Valley, is 450 miles long and 4,708 feet deep. It is the second deepest lake in the world.

In Kenya there are three large fresh-water lakes—Naivasha, Baringo and Rudolf; Uganda also has a number of fresh-water lakes such as Albert, George and Edward. Lake Victoria is so large (26,828 square miles—the size of Scotland) that it is like an inland sea, being partly in Kenya, Uganda and Tanzania. Lakes Tanganyika, Rukwa and Nyasa also contain fresh water, and are situated in the western and southern sections of the Rift Valley. All these fresh-water lakes abound with fish, and many support profitable commercial fishing enterprises as well as tribal and angling activities.

There are many different species of mouth-breeding tilapia fish living in African lakes; the species illustrated in this chapter is *Tilapia nigra*. The male nigra uses its mouth to clear pebbles away from a selected spot, making a basin-like depression on the bottom of the lake. He then jealously guards this "nest", and swims out to tempt each passing female into inspecting it. The female shows acceptance of the nest depression by tidying it up slightly, and this action greatly excites the male. As the female starts laying a stream of golden eggs, the dark male lies on his side to fertilize them as they settle on the bottom of the nest. The female then carefully gathers up the eggs in her mouth, the pharynx having become temporarily enlarged for this purpose. She then lays more eggs, and the whole process is repeated. After several hundred eggs have been laid and safely collected in the female's mouth, her whole appearance is altered by the bulging of her face. If the female does not swim away she will be chased off by the male, because he now wants the nest for his next wife.

During the period of incubation the female *Tilapia nigra* is not able to eat. After the fry hatch the mother continues to guard them, and for approximately ten days takes them into her mouth at the first sign of danger. The female in the photograph on page 268 hatched 782 young. When the female becomes tired of carrying her large brood in her mouth, she will slowly swim backwards while blowing out massed clouds of the little fish. Once in the water they stay very close to their mother, eager to swarm back into her mouth when danger threatens.

The alkaline lakes of the Rift Valley are inhospitable places, with noonday temperatures on the soda flats reaching 120° F or more. The high alkaline content of the water kills fish and mammals, but to some creatures it brings life. Microscopic plants—diatoms and blue-green algae—find the waters of these lakes, combined with abundant sunlight, a perfect habitat. Here they multiply in millions so that their combined weight would have to be measured in tons. Since plant life is the basis of all animal life, it is not surprising to find a creature which has adapted its way of life to reap a rich harvest from these alkaline lakes. The beautiful pink flamingoes live on these soda lakes of the Great Rift Valley, moving from one to another as conditions change. As the flamingoes fly to new areas at night, the flamingo population of a given lake may alter by several hundred thousand birds between one day and the next. Massed flamingoes present one of the most fantastic and colourful sights an ornithologist could hope to see.

In East Africa there are two species of flamingo, the lesser and the greater. The lesser flamingo is far more numerous. It feeds on the microscopic plants flourishing in the alkaline lakes and its highly specialized beak is designed for straining the minute blue-green algae and diatoms from the water. A flamingo feeds with its head held upside down in the water so that the upper mandible is lowermost. Its long neck swings the bird's head back and forth through the surface water with a rhythmic scything action. Lines of fine hairs cover the inside of each mandible and these act as filters, with the hairs rising and falling as the water flows in and out of the beak. The flamingo's tongue fits into a groove in the lower mandible and works like a piston in a pump to ensure a continuous flow of water through the filters. This marvellously adapted tongue has small backward-pointing protuberances which move the mass of strained algae and diatoms into the gullet, thereby making the straining and eating process continuous.

The greater flamingo, which feeds in a somewhat similar fashion, is more widespread in distribution than the lesser flamingo; it can be found from the Mediterranean coast of Europe to southern vleis in the Cape Province of South Africa. These birds often mingle with lesser flamingoes in the alkaline lakes of eastern Africa, but always in much smaller numbers. Their food consists of small crustaceans and the aquatic larvae of insects which they sieve from mud at the bottom of the lakes and coastal inlets. Because of their different food requirements, the greater flamingoes can live in fresh-water lakes as well as in soda lakes and coastal marshes.

The rich variety of bird life around the East African fresh-water lakes needs to be seen to be believed. Most of these lakes have resident populations of pelicans, marabous, herons, egrets, ibis, cormorants, darters, coots, grebes, Egyptian geese, ducks of many varieties, plovers, fish eagles and scores of other birds. The Great Rift Valley, with its chain of lakes, provides a flyway for birds migrating to southern Africa to escape the European winter. Some of the lakes, which have patches of forest around the shore, have an amazing variety of birds; four hundred different species have been recorded from the one small area.

Lake Edward, in the Queen Elizabeth National Park in western Uganda, is a paradise for birds, as well as for big game. Hippo Point, where many of the photographs illustrating this chapter were taken, is a peninsula two hundred yards long projecting into Lake Edward, sparsely dotted with clumps of bushes and euphorbia trees. On either side of Hippo Point large schools of hippos rest partly submerged in the water. Their guttural grunts can be heard throughout the day, while from the clear blue sky above a fish eagle, with head thrown back, calls melodiously to its mate perched on a spiny spire at the top of a euphorbia tree. A pied kingfisher hovers twenty feet above the water, then plunges headfirst into the lake to catch a small fish. Near the point, over a hundred great white pelicans assume varied grooming attitudes and their enormous beaks are rarely still as even the smallest of their feathers are straightened. Dotted amongst the pelicans are hundreds of other birds—cormorants and darters drying their wings, wattled and spurwing plovers, colourful wood ibis or painted storks, sacred and hadada ibises, herons and egrets, jacanas or lily trotters, ruffs, greenshanks and sandpipers of many species. Watching over the whole scene are fifty or more dignified marabou storks, their white body feathers contrasting with the dark grey of their wings and the reddish skin of their heads and throat pouches.

In the water the partly submerged hippos act as refuges for a variety of resting gulls, terns and other birds. For instance, a pair of jacanas, with an immature youngster, have learnt to fly out to the hippos to catch flies on their backs—even daring to stalk a wary fly settled on the bristly nose of a hippo. Watching the jacanas closely we found that they pecked the sores in the hippos' thick hide, drawing blood. From the hippos' reaction this obviously hurt. It was surprising to see a jacana drinking blood from a hippo—in the same way that a tick bird opens a sore on a resting rhinoceros. A variety of sandpipers, including the common, wood and marsh, stalked insects on the hippos' backs, but did not annoy their hosts. Cormorants and darters used the hippos as they would rocks—perfect resting places where they could dry their outstretched wings in the sunshine. Occasionally both Egyptian geese and wood ibis landed on the broad backs of the hippos, but flew off quickly when the hippos began to submerge. Cattle egrets often alight on hippos and stay for long periods—as shown by the white streaks on the animals' backs. We have filmed both the grey heron and numerous hammerkops using hippos as mobile frog-catching platforms. At another point in Lake Edward turtles climb on to the backs of partly submerged hippos, obviously finding this a safe sun-baking locality from which they can slip into deep water at the first sign of danger. We have also seen a monitor lizard climb right over the back of a partly submerged hippo, without the hippo taking the slightest notice.

The big concentration of hippos in Lake Edward benefits the birds in other ways. Each night the hippos leave the water to crop grass growing on the flats some distance away, returning to the lake before dawn. Because of the presence of thousands of hippos, literally tons of chewed-up grass in their excrement finds its way into the lake each day. This organic matter promotes plankton growth and not only helps to support a large fish population, but also aquatic insects of many species. Wave action brings the masticated grass to shore, where it is often piled several inches high. Flies and other insects breed in this decaying mass, and they, in turn, provide a source of food for thousands of insectivorous birds.

It is a strange sight on a sunny day to see a dark cloud moving across Lake Edward, changing its shape continuously. This is a living cloud of lake flies, which are small Chironomids no larger than a mosquito, but fortunately not capable of biting or stinging. When the wind blows them on to land they can be a nuisance, especially at night when myriads cluster around the lights. However, for other insects and birds the lake flies provide a food source of inestimable value, and no doubt contribute greatly to the abundance of bird life.

At the opposite end of the scale to the lake flies are the elephants which come to drink around the shore of Lake Edward. Walking in line astern down Hippo Point, they will pass amongst the pelicans and other waterbirds clustered near the point, the birds moving only a few feet out of the way to let the elephants pass. This is always a thrilling sight, and one not seen in many other areas of Africa. If the elephants move out into the water to drink and bathe, it is not unusual to see a raft of fishing pelicans swimming nearby.

There are two species of pelicans in Africa, the great white and the pink-backed; both nest in colonies, the former on the ground, the latter in trees. Although both species mix freely on shore while resting and grooming, each has a different method of feeding. The great white pelican is a community fisher, with many birds forming a raft in the water to drive the fish into the shallows. As the pelicans swim along they plunge their huge open beaks into the water in unison, turning at the same time to form a circle. Fish trying to escape from this trap use haste more than caution, and often swim straight into one of the wide open beak pouches. On catching a fish a great white pelican lifts its head high in the air to drain off the water, and manoeuvres its prey within the pouch so that it can be swallowed head first.

The pink-backed pelican is a lone fisher; individual birds work their favourite section of shallow water near shore. Floating almost motionless on the surface of the lake, a pink-backed pelican will plunge its open beak sideways into the water. It is rather surprising that this lone method of fishing works as well as it does.

While camped on Crescent Island, in Lake Naivasha, we witnessed an almost unbelievable sight. A marsh harrier was flying along the lakeshore when it attacked a squacco heron, knocking it into the lake. Circling around quickly, the marsh harrier swooped down to pick up the heron in its talons. But it was too heavy, and certainly still very much alive, so the two birds crash-landed into the water together. At this moment a pink-backed pelican flew in and landed nearby, just as the harrier took off and circled overhead. Then another pelican flew in from the left, and a third from the right. The squacco heron tried to take off and flapped along the surface of the lake for several yards before the weight of its saturated feathers caused it to fall exhausted into the water. Meanwhile the harrier circled low overhead, and the three pelicans swam alongside as if trying to protect the heron. While we watched through binoculars our friend, Hugo van Lawick, put a small rubber boat into the water to paddle out to the rescue. The three pelicans continued to swim around the stricken heron, while the wind and waves brought it closer to shore. As Hugo approached in the boat the pelicans took off. Picking the dripping squacco heron from the water, Hugo then paddled back to camp. The heron had a few small marks, but otherwise seemed uninjured. We put it into a large cardboard box to dry off, and kept it overnight. The following morning it was perfectly fit, and flew off along the lakeshore as if nothing had happened. We had not realized that a marsh harrier would attack a bird as large as a squacco heron and certainly, unless we had seen it with our own eyes, we would not have believed that pelicans would fly in to protect another species of bird. The marsh harrier could never be a threat to the pelicans, and there seems to be no logical explanation for their combined action in protecting the heron.

Dotted along the Great Rift Valley in eastern Africa is a chain of lakes. Some contain fresh water while others, with a high alkaline content, are called soda lakes. The picturesque fresh-water Lake Naivasha (above and preceding page) is lined with clumps of papyrus and yellow acacia trees. In western Uganda there are many attractive crater lakes (below) which reflect the distant Ruwenzori, the fabled "Mountains of the Moon".

From the Queen Elizabeth National Park in Uganda one can look across Lake Edward and watch the sun setting behind high mountains in the Congo. Lake Edward is probably as rich in bird and animal life as any lake in the world, and it certainly must have the greatest concentration of hippopotamuses of any lake.

A difficult problem—count the flamingoes! This is ▶▶ a dawn scene at Lake Nakuru, only 100 miles from Nairobi, when it was estimated that two million flamingos were on the lake. Most of the birds are sleeping, with their heads resting along their backs between their wings, and one leg folded up under their bodies.

No bird spectacle in the world can equal the sight ▶▶▶ of thousands of colourful flamingoes taking to the air on a sunny day.

Flamingoes do most of their feeding in shallow water; therefore few people realize that they are excellent swimmers, resembling swans when in deep water. To take off from the water a flamingo makes use of its webbed feet to gain speed by "running" along the surface, at the same time flapping its wings to get airborne. Right: the head of a lesser flamingo, showing the strange bill adapted for straining algae and tiny organisms from the water.

Four greater flamingoes close to avocets, black-tailed godwits and a stilt in the fresh-water shallows of Lake Naivasha. The greater flamingo has a deep pink bill, with a dark tip. Left: one of the flamingoes pauses to scratch its neck, showing how the leg is jointed in the opposite direction to our own knees.

There is always something enchanting about ▶ mother love in nature, and baby birds or animals have a charm of their own. These tiny goslings do not have a care in the world while under the watchful eye of their mother, an Egyptian goose.

Towards midday the sun is hot at Lake Baringo, ▶▶ Kenya, and the little goslings rest in the shade of their sleeping mother, while the watchful Egyptian gander does his turn of sentry duty.

An alert male defassa waterbuck stands at the edge of papyrus growing along the bank of the Nile in Uganda. Where papyrus is growing thickly it becomes impossible to reach the water unless a track is cut through the growth.

The edge of a luxuriant stand of papyrus, with ▶ vines climbing many of the stems. In the centre of a papyrus swamp the stems may be three inches in diameter, and twenty feet or more high. The papyrus plant grew profusely in Egypt before the Christian era, and the early Egyptians used papyrus to make a paper-like writing material. Now papyrus is almost extinct in Egypt, but it grows profusely in rivers and lakes of the Sudan, Uganda and Kenya.

The hippopotamus makes its home in and around the rivers and lakes of Africa, sleeping and resting by day in large schools like this one in Lake Edward. The bulky hippo is buoyant, and can submerge or rise to the surface at will.

A jacana, or lily trotter, has very long toes to support its weight evenly while walking on floating waterlily ▸ leaves, but it would be impossible for it to spread its weight evenly over the great expanse of this hippo's back.

The partly submerged hippos make perfect landing places for many species of waterbirds, like the tern about to alight behind the lesser blackbacked gulls, or the darter drying its wings.

When on land a hippo appears far too bulky to be supported by its relatively small legs and feet. Submerged in water a hippo is buoyant, but may actually weigh as much as two and a half tons. This is a lot, as a big hippo is under five feet high at the shoulder.

A quiet, sleepy school of hippos may suddenly erupt as two of the animals begin a noisy fight. With mouths agape, the antagonists try to make use of the sharp tusks in the lower jaw, to rip their opponent's body. Frightful wounds are sometimes inflicted and hippo quite often die as a result of fighting. However, much of the fighting in the water is friendly rivalry or even a type of love play between a male and a female, which is repeated at frequent intervals throughout the day. Overleaf: the large mouth and sharp teeth of a hippo show up clearly when it yawns. The tusks in the upper jaw are in fact the 'strops' which keep the long lower tusks almost razor sharp.

It is unusual to see a pair of Egyptian geese settled on the backs of partly submerged hippos.

Common sandpipers often spend time chasing flies across the broad expanse of a hippo's back.

The larger marsh sandpiper also visits a school of hippos in order to catch insects.

Cormorants use a hippo as they would a rock— as a place on which to dry off.

The grey heron finds that a hippo is slightly mobile while in the water, and is therefore a useful base for fishing.

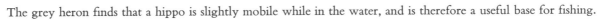

Hammerkops make use of hippos in still another way, as mobile frog-catching platforms. Each time the hippos move they disturb frogs from the muddy bottom, and when these surface to breathe, the hammerkops are ready and waiting. On catching a frog the hammerkop immediately flies to shore (below), where the frog is killed (right) and swallowed (left) Overleaf: the hammerkops do not disturb the hippos at all, as can be seen by this hippo sleeping with its chin resting on the back of another hippo.

The monitor lizard is a voracious predator equally at home on land or in the water. It will eat the eggs or chicks of ground nesting birds, frogs and even baby crocodiles. While swimming, a monitor may pass over or alongside a mud–caked hippo (below).

With its tiny tail flicking, a black crake moves across submerged vegetation as it returns to its nest in a clump of reeds.

Crowned cranes are large and beautiful birds, as ▶▶ graceful in flight as they are on the ground.

Crowned cranes are one of the most attractive African birds, sometimes congregating in large flocks during the non-breeding season. When the birds pair off there is much bowing and aerobatic manoeuvring as a climax to their dancing display. Each pair chooses an isolated nesting site, usually in tall grass or reeds on a small island surrounded by water. The birds take turns to incubate the eggs. The chicks leave the nest within a day or two and eagerly swallow the insects which they are fed while moving about. Even when the top-knot starts to develop, a chick still does not resemble its parents.

The cry of the fish eagle is one of the most musical and haunting sounds heard around the rivers and lakes of Africa. The birds are usually seen inpairs, ca lling to one another—with head thrown back—while flying as well as when settled. The fish eagle will sweep down over the water to snatch up a fish with its sharp talons, flying towards the sun so that its shadow does not frighten the intended victim. Below: at Lake Naivasha a fish eagle sits in a small thorn tree close to great white pelicans. Right: great white pelicans are a common sight around the lakes and, for such heavy birds, are graceful fliers.

Great white pelicans fly long distances between lakes, with sometimes as many as a thousand or more birds congregating in one place. They swim together and fish in large rafts, so as to herd a shoal of fish towards the shallows.

If fishing is successful other pelicans fly in to join the group. Plunging their heads beneath the water in unison the pelicans panic the fish so that some swim straight into the gaping pouches. Tilting its head up in the air a successful pelican swallows the fish.

A very unusual scene of a goliath heron spreading its wings to sun them on the underside, while resting on a partly submerged fence post.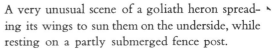

Before a goliath heron could swallow the tilapia it had caught, another heron also gripped the fish, starting a tug-of-war which lasted for many minutes.

There are several species of mouth-breeding tilapia living in the lakes of Africa, but their breeding habits vary greatly. A female *Tilapia nigra* is shown here taking the fry back into her mouth at the approach of danger. Already several hundred tiny fish are safely inside.

Tilapia are prolific breeders, and grow quickly in ▶ lakes where there is plenty of food in the form of plankton, aquatic plants and insect life. Fishing is a very good commercial business for many of the native tribes, as can be seen by this canoe full of fish at Lake Baringo, Kenya.

Where fish are plentiful the crocodile population ▶▶ of a lake will live almost entirely on them. A crocodile must lift its head clear of the water before swallowing its catch.

A dragonfly has just emerged and is drying its wings in the sun. A number of species of insects begin life as aquatic larvae, called nymphs, and many are eaten by fish while living in the water.

Marabou storks are scavengers and are usually ▶ found close to water, especially near fishing villages.

A marabou stork rests, with one foot clutching the other leg at the knee. The function of the pendulous neck pouch is not clearly understood as it is not connected to the gullet, but it can be inflated with air at will.

7 The Forest

The tropical rain forest of Africa is divided into two main sections, the larger of which is known as the Congo Forest. This covers a vast area, stretching from the Mountains of the Moon, which form Uganda's western boundary with the Congo, right across the vast Congo River basin to the Atlantic Ocean in the west, and extending north to Gabon, the Cameroons and the narrow coastal strip of south-eastern Nigeria. The smaller tract is known as the Upper Guinea Forest, and covers the coastal lowlands of West Africa from Sierra Leone to Ghana.

A few thousand years ago the tropical rain forest belt extended much further than it does today. Small pockets of this great rain forest still exist in East Africa and are inhabited by typically West African mammals and birds; they are islands of West African flora and fauna surviving in the east and as such are of particular interest to zoologists and botanists. The bongo is the largest mammal that has become isolated in forest pockets in Kenya, but there are many smaller species such as the potto, the scaly-tailed gliding squirrel and the brush-tailed porcupine.

Looking down on a rain forest from an aeroplane one sees a sea of green, with a canopy of the trees forming an unbroken carpet 120 feet or more above the ground. So uniform in height are these huge forest trees that one is not aware of the individual trees in the rain forest, but only of the slight undulations of the green canopy. Seen from the forest floor, one gets a totally different picture of the region. The ground is carpeted with a thick layer of dead and decaying leaves; small bushes are numerous, and their thick foliage greatly restricts eye-level visibility. The straight stems of young trees extend above the bushes, their leaves forming an intermediate level in the forest about thirty to sixty feet above the ground. The real forest giants have enormous buttresses, with many flanges spreading the weight of the tree over a considerable area of ground; these are essential because the big forest trees lack strong tap roots.

Animal life in this habitat has adapted itself to the various levels of the forest. Many species live their entire lives in and around the canopy, the interwoven branches of which form aerial highways for monkeys, pottos, and squirrels. Numerous birds, as well as many species of insects, also remain in this uppermost layer. Some creatures prefer to live below the canopy, others dwell on the ground, and still others make up an interesting world of life beneath the carpet of dead leaves on the ground.

The rain forest is the home of many varieties of monkeys. Their passage through the trees can more often be followed by the swaying branches than by the sight of the animals themselves, but sometimes they may be seen leaping, one after the other, from the same high branch to a nearby tree. The most spectacular aerial artist is the black and white colobus, which can easily jump a gap of twenty to thirty feet, with its long white mantle flowing majestically in the breeze.

It is very difficult to see any of the animals in the rain forest and virtually impossible to photograph the larger creatures in the natural state. A waterhole or natural saltlick offers the best hope for photography. The discovery of such a spot in the Aberdares in Kenya led to the construction of Treetops; a hotel built in trees overlooking a waterhole. Treetops has a flat roof for game viewing, as well as two lower floors each of which has a darkened verandah where visitors can sit in comfortable, aircraft-type reclining chairs. The waterhole which lies in front of the Hotel is a hundred yards or more across, and is partly covered with waterlilies and reeds. Here a keen bird watcher is sure to list quite a number of African birds seen in the natural state—coot, dabchick, duck, teal, herons, egrets, and even crowned cranes which nest each year towards the centre of the reeds. Usually there are many warthogs around the grassy verge of the forest, as well as waterbuck and bushbuck.

At the saltlick, olive baboons move freely amongst the bushbuck and some of the younger ones often tease the antelope. One may well see a baboon casually move up behind a bushbuck, hit it on the flank or hindleg with a flick of its hand, and run away before the bushbuck has a chance to retaliate. This game is often repeated, and the adolescent baboons also tease young warthogs in the same way. A troop of baboons usually times its arrival at the waterhole to coincide with the serving of afternoon tea at the Hotel, and the baboons eagerly catch pieces of cake thrown to them.

Tourists are always particularly keen to see buffalo, rhinoceros and—the animal species which thrills them most—elephants. To a keen naturalist, however, it will be of more interest to see giant forest hogs for the first time, though to a layman these may seem like a family of very large domestic pigs. The giant forest hog was not discovered until 1904 and, as its name implies, it is only found in thick forests. The general body colour is blackish-grey and it is covered with long, coarse hairs. From a distance the giant forest hog does resemble a large domestic pig, but the males, which weigh as much as 550 pounds, have extraordinary facial protuberances below their eyes. Semicircular in shape, these jut out from the face like half plates, and are far more weird-looking than the knobbly protuberances of a warthog.

With so many species of animals competing for space at the saltlick, or mingling around the waterhole, it is not surprising that visitors to Treetops often witness interesting scenes of animal behaviour. One very unusual incident occurred late on the afternoon of February 20th, 1963. A few weeks earlier the resident pair of crowned cranes had successfully hatched three chicks, which each day followed their parents in search of insects to eat. On this particular day a herd of elephants arrived, passing close to the cranes. Two elephants, the equivalent of human teenagers, decided to chase the cranes. Because of the difference in size this should have been a rout, but the adult cranes stood their ground, calling loudly, with their black and white wings outstretched. Surprised by this brave reaction the elephants stopped short, their trunks swinging up in the air in defiance. Slowly the cranes tried to edge past towards the water, but one or other of the elephants would always run in, trumpeting loudly. The cranes would not leave the flightless chicks, but tried to guide them away from the danger. One of the elephants shook a tree, finally ripping off a small branch which it hurled towards the cranes. For twenty minutes the dispute continued, accompanied by almost unbelievable sound effects. Finally the cranes reached the waterhole with two of the chicks, and moved out to the nest in the reeds. The male then took off, calling loudly as he circled the waterhole three times before landing in the grass where the encounter with the elephants had taken place. It was obvious that he was looking for the missing chick, which must have been trampled to death by one of the elephants. The male crane stayed near this spot until it was quite dark, then flew back to the nest to rejoin the other members of his family. Most birds cannot count, but these cranes certainly knew that one chick was missing.

It is usually well after dark before the main concentration of animals at the waterhole and salt-lick takes place. One large electric light, resembling the moon, shines over the waterhole throughout the night, and the animals have become accustomed to this artificial moonlight. The rhinos arrive singly, except for females followed by their youngsters; after drinking noisily, they claim part of the saltlick as their territory. A rhinoceros seems to be constantly on edge, and while at the saltlick will often squeal, making a high-pitched sound which one would associate with any other animal but a rhino. When charging other animals they also huff and puff like a locomotive engine. If a dozen or more rhinos are scattered around the saltlick during the night, they make so much continuous noise that few people at Treetops are able to sleep. However, a few hours before dawn the rhinos begin to disperse, moving off singly into the forest. By dawn the whole area is usually deserted.

The magnificent bongo is the largest forest-dwelling species of antelope; occasionally in the middle of the night it makes an appearance at Treetops. Both sexes carry horns, of similar shape but more massive in size than those of a male bushbuck. The colouring is a deep reddish-brown, with older males turning a dark mahogany. The body is marked with between eleven and thirteen vertical white stripes, often with one more stripe on one side of the body than on the other. Along the ridge of the back, bongos have a mane which can be fully erected when the animal is alarmed or otherwise excited. This is far more pronounced than the crest sometimes erected by the much smaller bushbuck.

The bongo is by far the largest forest-dwelling antelope while the little West African royal antelope is the smallest species of antelope in the world. The East African suni is another very small forest antelope, having pencil-thin legs and tiny hoofs no larger than a man's thumbnail. There are at least ten species of duiker living in the rain forest; they are therefore the most plentiful type of antelope in this habitat. All duikers are browsers, sometimes standing up on their hind legs amongst the bushes to reach higher leaves. Many of the forest duikers are deep reddish-brown in colour, with blackish faces. The zebra duiker, which lives in West African forests, has dark vertical markings on its body.

The Pygmies are efficient hunters of the Ituri Forest, spreading rope nets through the under-growth to capture a number of different animals. The most common species caught is the little blue duiker, which they call Boloko. They also capture red duiker, the large yellow-backed duiker, and the spotted water chevrotain. The okapi lives in the Ituri Forest in the eastern Congo, and for centuries has been hunted by the Pygmies. Although it is a large animal related to the giraffe, it was not discovered by Europeans until 1900.

Some years before independence, the Belgian Administration established an Okapi Capturing Station at Epulu, where the main road from Stanleyville north through the Ituri Forest crosses the Epulu River. Two hundred deep pits were dug on forest trails, and when an okapi fell into a pit an ingenious method was used to move the animal to Epulu with the least possible shock. Two parallel stick fences were made from the pit to the nearest track, and at this point an earthen ramp was made up to the level of the back of a lorry, which had a natural-looking pen built on to it in advance. When all was ready one end of the pit was dug away, so that the shy okapi could walk up the incline unaided, then along the fenced track and on to the truck. When the lorry arrived at the Epulu Capturing Station a similar system of twin stake fences was employed to allow the okapi to walk into its new enclosure, built in natural forest. Many of the leading zoos throughout the world now have a pair of okapis, caught at Epulu, and they are being successfully bred in captivity.

At wet patches by the side of the road near Epulu, butterflies settle to suck moisture direct from the soil. The many species of gorgeously coloured Charaxes butterflies also congregate at animal droppings on the road, and here they are joined by a variety of tiny blues and brown ringlets. One day near Epulu a venomous puff adder had been run over and squashed on the road, and a great variety of butterflies clustered around the dead snake, sucking its body fluids. Not all forest butterflies have this strange taste, but the ones that do are often more brilliantly marked than those which sip nectar from flowers.

Birds of the rain forest are often spectacularly coloured. Many species, however, are more frequently heard than seen. The touracos are spectacular large birds, often coloured bright green, with the flight feathers a brilliant red, but these are only noticeable when the bird flies or glides between trees. The touraco has a habit of hopping rapidly along the branches of some giant forest tree, working higher all the time. Then from a vantage point it glides quite a long way to another tree, where the process of hopping up through the branches is repeated. The giant blue touraco is quite common in patches of forest in Uganda, and its loud staccato call is frequently heard before sunset as the big birds move to their favourite roosting trees. The large black and white hornbills are also noisy dwellers of the high forest trees, and their heavy-flapping wingbeats can often be heard even if the cover is too thick to see the actual birds.

The largest of the forest predators is the leopard; the lion and the cheetah never venture into this type of environment, and even the leopard seems to prefer forests where there is open country nearby. The golden cat is an interesting feline of the thick rain forests. In the Congo it appears in three totally different colour phases—one a rich chestnut-red colour typical of the golden cat; another type a bluish-grey like a puma; and there is also a melanistic form with a deep-black coat. A smaller predator of the rain forest is the sleek and agile genet. Although commonly called the genet cat, it is related to the mongooses and civets. The large and handsomely marked tiger genet is found in the Congo Forest, as well as some of the smaller species of genets common in East Africa. The genet preys on birds, small mammals, lizards and insects.

The rain forest does not have the big mammalian scavengers which keep the plains clean, but the smaller creatures of the forest are every bit as efficient. A big proportion of the scavengers of the rain forest are insects, other arthropods and bacteria. These not only cope efficiently with the break-up of animal matter, but the even more important task of coping with the build-up of dead leaves, twigs and branches. In the damp environment of the forest floor the small scavengers quickly decompose this debris, at the same time enriching the soil for new growth. Nowhere is growth more rapid and abundant than in the rain forest, and it is indeed an exciting place to visit if one is interested in natural history.

Animal life in this habitat has adapted to the various levels of the forest, with many species living in and around the canopy, without descending to the ground. Although a wealth of wildlife lives in a rain forest, it is almost impossible to see it because of the thick vegetation.

IN THIS ꓥꓮꓲꓲꓟꓴ TREE

HER ROYAL HIGHNESS THE PRINCESS ELIZABETH

AND

HIS ROYAL HIGHNESS THE DUKE OF EDINBURGH

SPENT THE NIGHT OF FEBRUARY 5th., 1952

WHILE HERE PRINCESS ELIZABETH

SUCCEEDED TO THE THRONE THROUGH

THE DEATH OF HER FATHER

KING GEORGE THE SIXTH

By attracting the shy forest creatures into a clearing it is possible to watch them, and this is why Treetops in Kenya has become famous for game viewing; situated in the Aberdares National Park, not far from the township of Nyeri, it is a little over 100 miles north of Nairobi. There is a large waterhole just in front of Treetops, but in this mountainous area there are also many streams where the animals can drink. Long before Treetops was built the animals visited the waterhole because it was also the site of a natural saltlick. Now, each day before the tourists arrive at Treetops, salt is scattered over the ground close to the building. Not only do the animals come to drink, but they spend many hours at the saltlick, drinking again before they return to the surrounding forest.

Some time after the Royal visitors spent a night at Treetops in 1952, the original hotel, built in a large *mgumu*, or wild fig tree, was destroyed by fire. Several years elapsed before the new Treetops was constructed, as shown above, and more recently the sleeping accommodation has been increased.

Waterbuck can usually be seen within the forest clearing at Treetops, and the males spend a lot of time practising the art of fighting, like schoolboys learning to wrestle. Fighting is an acquired skill, even with animals, and it takes years of practice to become proficient enough to take over a harem and guard it against usurping males.

A female waterbuck pauses to drink at the edge of the forest. ▸

A pair of bushbuck and a big baboon at the Treetops saltlick. Male bushbuck vary in colour from dark reddish-brown to almost black, while females are a much lighter reddish-brown, often spotted with white. Olive baboons are regular visitors, pausing to drink before moving close to the building where the human visitors are having afternoon tea.

This young male baboon has climbed a tree, and is hopefully waiting for a piece of cake to be thrown to him; hence the look of eager expectation on his face.

A general view across waterlilies and reeds to ▸▸ where buffalo are drinking.

285

This old bull buffalo had obviously been enjoy- ▸▸▸ ing a mudbath before coming to the saltlick.

For a naturalist it is a thrilling sight to see giant forest hogs for the first time, but the average tourist at Treetops hardly gives them a second glance. The elusive giant forest hog was not discovered until 1904. Old males weigh up to five hundred pounds and have large protuberances beneath the eyes, as can be seen on the big boar at the rear of the group. A tiny piglet is just visible in the front row, behind two larger youngsters. Warthogs (right) are more common than giant forest hogs, and can be seen each day at Treetops without fail. Giant forest hogs are not so regular and usually come late at night.

A large herd of elephants leaves the forest in daylight, walking in single file towards ▶▶
a drinking spot just below the game viewing platforms.

After drinking, the elephants congregate at the saltlick within easy camera range. ▶▶▶

An old bull elephant waded into the waterhole to eat the succulent water plants. ▶▶▶▶

A pair of crowned cranes hatched three chicks among the reeds near the centre of the waterhole at Treetops. A natural drama took place late on the afternoon of February 20th, 1963, when the cranes were taking their chicks back to the nest to sleep for the night. An immature bull elephant chased the cranes for over half an hour, trumpeting and shaking bushes, and apparently trampling one chick to death.

With the coming of nightfall there is a change at Treetops. Baboons, warthogs and waterbuck disappear into the forest to sleep, but bushbuck continue to visit the saltlick throughout the night. Human visitors move to the spacious dining room to enjoy the evening meal.

Even when in bed at Treetops one is made aware of being high up in the trees by the living branch growing through the wall. A game scout is on duty throughout the night, and visitors can arrange to be called should an interesting animal visit the saltlick. Treetops is perhaps the only place in Africa where that rare antelope the bongo may sometimes be seen, usually late at night.

Elephants visit Treetops more often at night than ▶▶ during the day, and a flashlight photograph captures this herd on film when they pause at the saltlick.

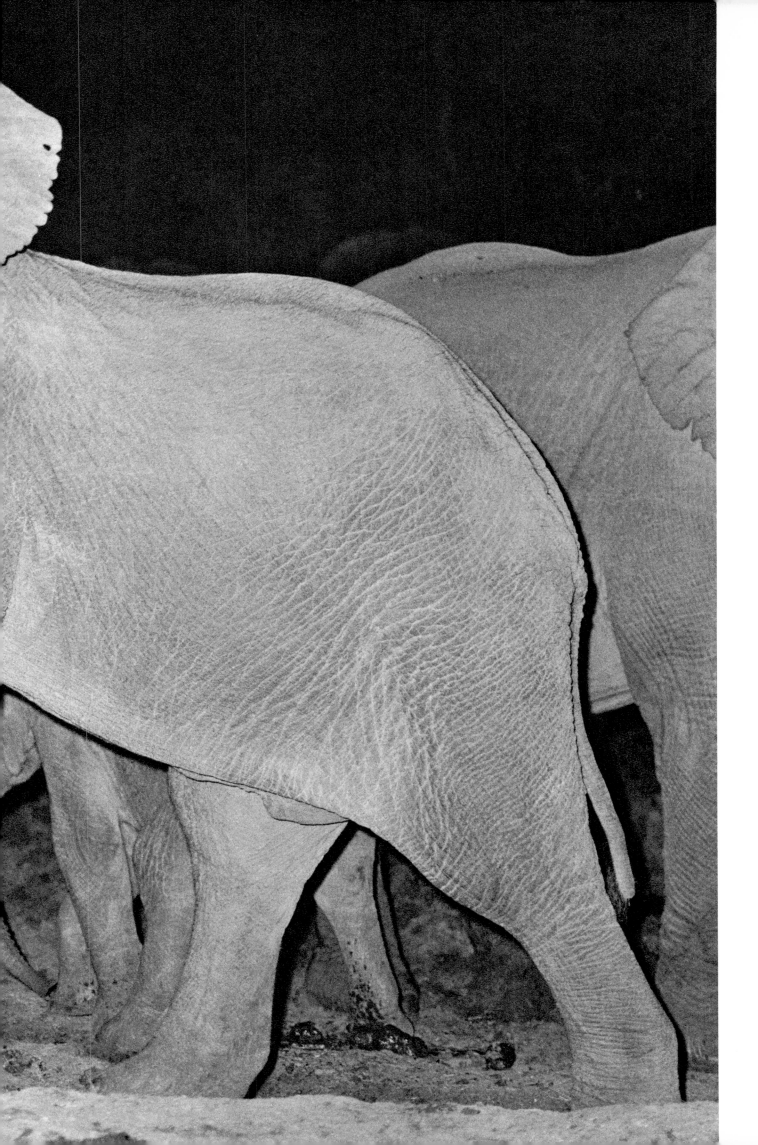

The truculent rhinoceros comes to the saltlick at night, noisily proclaiming its right to a particular spot and always ready to defend it against other animals, such as buffalo. Right, top: a rhino moves out of the mud at the edge of the water-hole, with the eyes of buffalo shining brightly in the background. Right, an elephant and a rhino approach each other apprehensively.

At midnight there may be many rhinos at the saltlick, as well as buffalo and bushbuck, but by dawn the saltlick is usually ▸▸ deserted—the nocturnal creatures having retired to the forest and the diurnal animals not yet awake and about.

The forests of Africa are wonderful places for colourful butterflies, particularly in clearings where they flit about before they settle, often with wings opened wide in the sun. These beautiful insects display a wide variety of shapes, with bold markings and a blending of colours unequalled by the best artists and dress designers.

Top left: A short tail admiral *(Antartia dimorphica howarth).*

Top right: Hannington's fritillary *(Issoria hanningtoni elwes).*

Below: a leaf butterfly *(Precis tugela).*   Right: The striking markings of the African map *(Cyrestis camillus),* enlarged about three times, show clearly as two perfect specimens suck moisture from the wet gravel at the edge of a forest stream in Uganda.

◄ Having eaten the leaves at the end of a branch this oleander hawkmoth caterpillar (Daphnis nerii) rests with its real head curled under, displaying a large false eye mark on its body.

This six-inch praying mantis from Uganda (Hemiempusa capensis) has an extremely long and thin thorax. The front pair of legs, which are in reality efficient insect capturing arms, are folded in the characteristic "praying" position.

The mottled pink, mauve and green of this praying mantis nymph (Pseudocreobatra wahlbergii) blend with the colouring of flowers so as to render the insect almost invisible. Insects visiting the flowers for nectar are likely to be caught and eaten by the young mantis.

◄ This young male forest hornbill has a large casque on its beak, and although this looks very heavy, it is in fact amazingly light as the inside is honeycombed with air spaces.

A mousebird alights on its nest, with the long tail feathers still caught up in the branches. The two large chicks are almost ready to leave the nest, but it will take weeks for their tail feathers to grow fully.

There are many species of chameleons living in the forests, and when seen in close-up the head of a chameleon resembles a weird prehistoric monster.

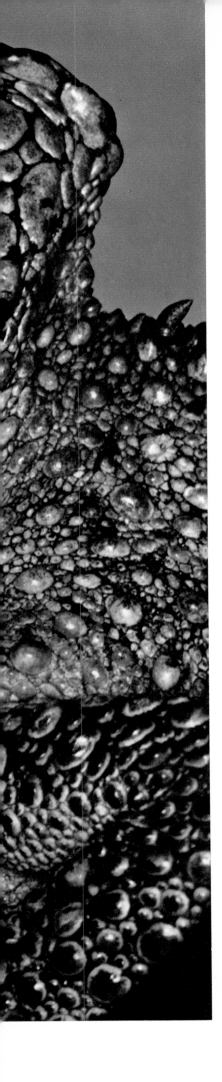

Three male chameleons, showing how much they differ: *bitaeniatus höhneli*, *jacksoni* and *fischeri*.

The "hands" of a chameleon appear grotesque when magnified, like medieval armour ▶▶

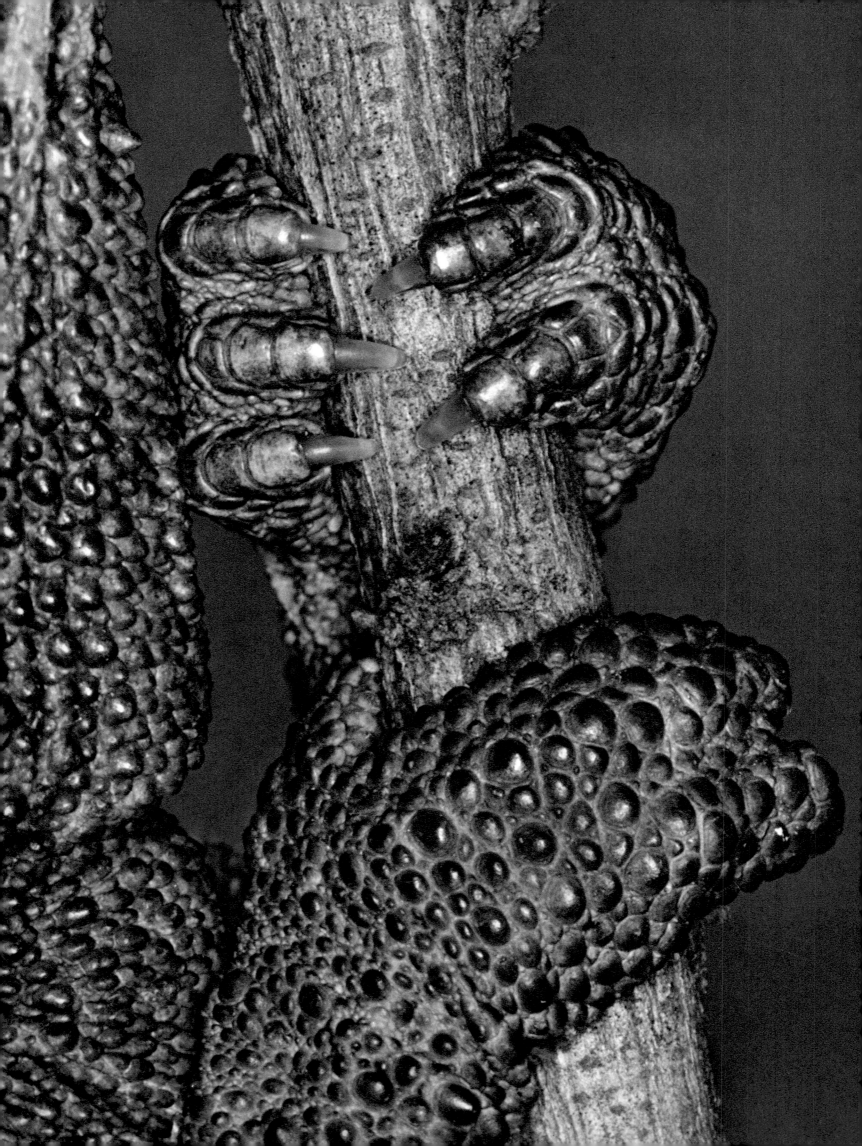

The potto is a strange looking nocturnal animal of the tropical forests. It is rarely seen as it spends the day sleeping, curled up in a tight furry ball high in a tree.

The forest-dwelling tree hyrax is more often heard than seen, having a particularly loud medley of harsh calls uttered only at night. It is a vegetarian, and is very fond of the leaves of wild fig trees.

The forest bushbaby is considerably larger than the little moholi bushbaby of the dry thornbush country, but its habits are much the same. It is active at night, jumping about in trees with great agility, searching for fruits, insects and even small sleeping birds.

The tiny royal antelope is the smallest antelope, standing only ten inches high at the shoulder. It lives in the forests of West Africa and the Congo.

The common bush duiker lives in thickets in fairly open country as well as in forests, eating leaves and also grasses.

The bongo is a large antelope living in the thick forests of West Africa and the Congo. It also inhabits belts of highland forest in Kenya.

Undiscovered until the beginning of this century, the okapi lives a secluded life in the Ituri Forest of the Congo. It is a member of the giraffe family, feeding on leaves, and has a prehensile upper lip as well as a very long tongue used to reach high foliage. The okapi's tongue is really amazing as it is able to lick behind the ears—a feat few animals can achieve. The body colour is a dark purplish-brown, the legs and rump being marked with white stripes.

The mountain gorilla's habitat is in the forests ▶ of the eastern Congo, and considerable numbers live on the Virunga volcanic group of mountains bordering southern Uganda.

The leopard is amazingly adaptable, living on the plains, in dry thornbush country, open bush and woodland, in thick forests and high on mountain ranges. In south-western Uganda it was discovered that a large leopard was gradually killing off a family of mountain gorillas—an almost unbelievable feat.

8 Snow on the Equator

The impression of Africa created by Tarzan-type movies and adventure books is one of hot and steamy jungles. Nothing could be further from the truth. Most of the animals of Africa are seen on the open plains, and not in jungles. Nearly all these game plains are on a high central plateau with an elevation of between three and six thousand feet, and although the days may be hot the nights are decidedly cool. A number of mountain ranges and individual peaks rise from this central plateau. Mount Kilimanjaro, Mount Kenya and the Ruwenzori Range—the fabled "Mountains of the Moon"—all three are very close to the equator, and yet are the only mountains in Africa with permanent ice, snow and glaciers.

Because the mountains in East Africa rise from a high plateau they do not appear to be very high—as compared to mountains of similar elevation near the coast. Kilimanjaro, Africa's highest mountain, is perhaps the most spectacular as its volcanic cone is of classical shape and looks somewhat like Japan's famous Mount Fujiyama. Mount Kenya is the second highest mountain in Africa; it is much older than Kibo (the snow-capped dome of Kilimanjaro) and has eroded greatly since the distant days when it was an active volcano. Mount Kenya rises from plains which have an elevation of 6,000 feet, and the extensive foothills tend to diminish the visual effect of the size of the twin peaks of Batian and Nelion, which are both just over 17,000 feet high. The vast and rugged Ruwenzori Mountains are hidden behind smoke haze for many months of the year, but in April and November, during the rains, they show up clearly. So vast are the foothills here that the snowfields look insignificant when viewed from the plains below. But if one climbs the Ruwenzori one is awed by its vastness.

Most people are surprised to hear of snow at the equator, for this is rightly regarded as the hottest region on earth. However, temperature throughout the world is governed by a number of factors, and elevation is perhaps the most influential for places having the same latitude.

Mount Kenya has a lot of character—if this can be said of a mountain—and it looks quite different when seen from different points. Even when there is not a cloud in the sky, the shadows move and viewing conditions change at each hour of the day. Very few days are cloudless, and it is usual for clouds to build up around the summit towards mid-morning, when strong winds blow the mists out from the peaks like an ever-moving white pennant. It is always fascinating to watch the birth of a cloud, and there are few places where this can be seen more effectively than on Mount Kenya. Some days the clouds build up, constantly changing shape as they grow, only to disperse rapidly as conditions alter in the rarefied air at 17,000 feet. Time-lapse cine photography speeds up the whole process and the effects of the strong eddying winds can be clearly seen from the cloud formation.

People living near the base of Mount Kenya find that they are never bored with the view of the mountain, for it changes all the time. Mr. Raymond Hook has farmed close to Mount Kenya for more than fifty years and he has probably spent more time exploring the mountain than any other person. Years ago he began to look on it as "my Mountain". Mountain climbers and members of scientific expeditions usually contact him when they plan a trip up Mount Kenya, as he can supply pack animals to deliver food and equipment right up to the snowline.

For many years he used mules as pack animals, though recently he has used trained zebroids as well. His zebroids all have the same Grevy's zebra stallion father, but different mares as their mothers. They retain the body colouring of the horse, but the stripes of the zebra. Some are therefore chestnut, others various shades of brown and some almost black. Like a mule, a zebroid is sterile. Running wild, a zebra is very sure-footed and has plenty of stamina; the zebroids retain these characteristics, and yet can be trained for work like a horse.

There are a number of well-recognized routes up Mount Kenya, all slightly different although each passes through similar zones of vegetation. The lower slopes are clothed in forest and are inhabited by many of the animals mentioned in the previous chapter—elephant, black rhinoceros, buffalo, bushbuck, bongo, duiker, suni, leopard, serval, bush pig, giant forest hog, colobus monkey, blue monkey, bushbaby, crested rat, giant forest rat, and many other creatures. The passage of the large mammals through the mountain forest keeps numerous tracks open, and as the ground underfoot is usually muddy it bears the footprints of the different animals using the trails. Large stands of cedar trees are festooned with long pendants of lichen, often called Spanish moss, or old man's beard, which is a very apt description. Growing amongst the cedars are many giant podocarpus trees, a member of the yew family, primitive conifers with spreading crowns and huge boles. These forest giants give the impression of great age, and it is awe-inspiring to look up into their lofty branches.

The forest on the lower slopes of Mount Kenya is more open than the typical rain forest, and its small glades are carpeted with grass and attractive ferns. Here, when the sun is shining, even though the elevation may be nine thousand feet, butterflies are active and the faint but distinct buzz from a carpenter bee visiting flowers several yards away can be clearly heard. The absence of bird sounds is noticeable, although a flycatcher may flit nearby without showing fear and the snap of its beak is clearly audible as it catches an insect on the wing.

Climbing higher one enters the bamboo forest belt, which has an eerie atmosphere of its own. The bamboos grow up to 40 feet in height and the ground is carpeted with their dead leaves. The wind rattles their hollow stems, making a creaking and crackling sound never heard elsewhere. As many of the bamboo stems are dead and broken, the wind blowing across their hollow ends produces a moaning sound. This is an interesting region for a brief visit, but it can be nerve-racking if one has to spend a long time in the bamboo forest. Elephant and buffalo live in this area, keeping trails open. The buffalo are usually shy, and a herd makes a great deal of noise as it runs off through the bamboo—crashing into the stems, which bang together and no doubt increase the fear of the fleeing animals. As in the lower forest there are grassy glades amongst the bamboos, usually along the ridges, providing the buffalo with good grazing. Crystal-clear mountain water cascades over rocks in the streams which run swiftly down the gullies. Here within a relatively small area the big animals have everything they need to make life pleasant.

Towards its upper limit the bamboo forest opens out into more grassy glades, where there are stunted bushes. As one continues to climb this region in its turn changes into more open country with giant heaths, which mark the beginning of the moorland. At this elevation (of about 11,000 feet) misty rain falls nearly every day. Colourful mosses and lichens cover the rocks, forming a thick carpet in the shade beneath the giant heaths. In cold northern countries, heaths grow no more than two or three feet high, but on the high mountains of East Africa they reach thirty feet or more in height. Their dead branches make excellent firewood for cooking and for warmth. The nights are very cold up here, and by morning frost covers the ground. Nevertheless a great variety of wild flowers may be seen throughout the year. The hardy Helichrysum, or everlasting, grows on the moorland, its flowers ranging from white to pink, with the deep yellow-orange centres attracting a variety of flies, wasps and butterflies.

The moorland is often soggy and covered mainly by clumps of tussocky grasses and hardy sedges. When elephants move across the moorland they often make deep imprints which fill with water and provide drinking water for man and beast alike. Buffalo also come out on to the open moorland quite regularly, and some have even wandered so high that their frozen bodies have remained intact for years at 16,000 feet. Accidents befall other animals also. "Icy Mike" was the name bestowed on a frozen elephant found high on Mount Kenya, while a leopard found frozen on Kilimanjaro at an even greater altitude fired the fancy of newspaper editors some years ago. This frozen leopard also captured the imagination of Ernest Hemingway, featuring in some of his African stories.

Leopards are not the only predators to venture out on to the moorland of East Africa's high mountains, for the serval hunts mole rats and other rodents above the forest line. Many rodents flourish as high as thirteen and fourteen thousand feet, and build regular tracks through the tussocky grass. Buzzards circle overhead by day, and at night the large Mackinder's eagle owl can be seen sitting on high rocks in the moonlight. Each rocky outcrop is the home of numerous hyraxes, which have much thicker fur than their relatives living on rocky kopjes on the plains. The plentiful supply of hyraxes no doubt explains the good physical condition of a pack of wild dogs seen in the snow at over 15,000 feet on Mount Kenya. On Kilimanjaro a similar pack was seen at over 19,000 feet.

Climbing higher on Mount Kenya's moorland one enters an unreal world where strange-looking plants add a bizarre touch to the harsh rocky landscapes and the spectacular views of mountain peaks and permanent snowfields. Here the unique flora of the high African mountains, the giant lobelias and giant groundsels, or senecios, grow in profusion amongst the tussocky grass and rocky outcrops. Because of the low temperatures, these giant plants grow very slowly; some of the larger specimens of senecios may well be two hundred years old. They first appear as a low rosette of leaves, and thirty years may pass before the woody shoot, covered with the plant's first blossoms, emerges from the centre. This three-foot flower stalk can be seen in the colour photograph on page 335. After the yellow flowers die, one or two side stalks will form rosettes of their own, and these give rise to the branched appearance of the mature plant. The giant lobelia also begins life as a rosette of tightly packed leaves, but these are more elongated and more numerous than the leaves of the groundsel, resembling a giant garden artichoke (page 334). As the lobelia grows, a broad central stem develops to a height of six or eight feet. The individual flowers are blue in colour, of insignificant size, and almost completely hidden behind long greenish-purple bracts, or leaves. The flower spike is spectacular because of its size, but the flowers themselves are not impressive. Flowering continues for a long period, and the scarlet-tufted malachite sunbird is a daily visitor as it sips nectar from each tiny blossom. This brilliant, long-tailed, emerald-green sunbird lives high on the East African mountains amongst the giant groundsels and giant lobelias, seldom venturing below 12,000 feet.

Higher on Mount Kenya, where snow lies for long periods, plant life cannot exist except in the form of hardy lichens which cling to the rocks. The Curling Pond, at an altitude of 15,700 feet, is permanently frozen, and the ice so thick that there was no danger of the zebroids and mules breaking through when they walked across it to off-load our supplies. The animals seem to retain remarkable stamina even at this altitude, but their stay was a short one—after only half an hour they were on their way down the mountain to spend the night on the moorland where grazing would be adequate.

Mount Kilimanjaro captures the imagination of everyone. To see game animals in the foreground and Kili's snow-capped summit in the background, is perhaps the most thrilling of all African panoramas. When camping one always wonders anxiously: "Will the mountain be clear tomorrow?" Waking during the night, one is apt to peer out through the open tent-flaps, past the silhouettes of thorn trees to the mountain showing clearly in the moonlight, with small silvery clouds lighting up the dark sky. Lions grunt in the distance and one settles down again with the thought: this really is Africa!

Before dawn the alarm clock rings. As the air is cold one dresses warmly and hurries out for a first look at the mountain. The sky is already growing light and the massive outline of Kilimanjaro stands out against the silvery-blue sky. A chorus of birds is welcoming the new day but nightjars are still about catching insects on the wing. Soon, equipped with cameras and binoculars, one is bouncing across country in the safari car trying to find the lions that called the evening before. Whether this is one's first trip to photograph wildlife or one's thousandth, there is the same feeling of excitement. It is impossible to know what dramatic scene will unfold when the next bush is passed. The longer one lives among wildlife the more one learns, and the more one learns the more one gains from each and every experience, and from the sheer joy of being in the bush in Africa.

Relatively few people climb to the summit of Kilimanjaro. To do so involves plodding steadily upwards, camping for three nights. On the way one may rest on a hard rock, legs stiff with fatigue and stiffening still more from sitting for a few minutes. On looking over the plains, with clouds forming below at an altitude of 16,000 feet, one wonders: "Will I ever be able to make it?" There is only one way to find out! And that is by keeping going.

Not everyone can climb to the summit, but those who do so stand on the roof of Africa, 19,340 feet above sea level. It is an unforgettable and awe-inspiring experience!

Mount Kenya has a very distinctive snow-capped peak, visible from many miles away on a clear day. This particular view, with a flowering Cape chestnut tree in the foreground, was taken from Treetops.

From thirty miles away it appears to be suspended between two layers of early morning cloud. ▶▶

The home of farmer and naturalist Raymond Hook, who is an authority on the wildlife of Mount Kenya. ▶▶▶

On his farm zebroids, a cross between horse and zebra, are rounded up to carry supplies up the mountain. ▶▶▶▶

An early morning scene in the bamboo forest, after an overnight camp on the slopes of Mount Kenya at an altitude of 9,000 feet.

Sunlight filtering through the giant bamboos ▶ lights up smoke from the cooking fire in the cold early morning air.

The symmetrical leaves of a young lobelia resemble an artichoke's formation. The centre of the
giant lobelia grows upwards, as a tall flower spike,
to a height of seven or eight feet.

Another characteristic plant of the high alpine
regions of East Africa is the giant groundsel or
senecio. It grows very slowly, at high altitudes up
to almost 15,000 feet, but it is seldom photographed
when flowering. This is not surprising, as it takes
approximately thirty years before a three-foot
woody shoot emerges to carry the plant's first
blossom.

Leopards sometimes live high in the mountains, venturing up to 15,000 feet and more, apparently not greatly worried by the cold. They stalk duiker on the moorland just above the forest line, but range even higher, hunting hyraxes among the rocky outcrops.

The serval cat also lives on the high mountains of East Africa, hunting the many species of rodents which make tunnels through the tussocky grasses on the moorland. When the serval is resting its spotted coat blends perfectly with the surroundings.

Hyraxes live high on the mountains of East Africa, where sudden storms may leave behind a carpeting of snow. Here, at an elevation of 13,000 to 14,000 feet, the hardy hyraxes grow long, thick fur, but enjoy sitting in the sun whenever possible. When the rock hyrax yawns, its long canine teeth show up clearly.

Mackinder's eagle owl is not uncommon in the ▶ East African highlands, though it was once considered to be extremely rare. With the abundance of rodents it has no difficulty in hunting, even as high as 14,000 feet near Two Tarn hut on Mount Kenya.

Clouds swirl around Mount Kenya's summit (17,058 feet) as the pack animals arrive at Hut Tarn to be unloaded.

The snow-covered heights of Mount Kenya seen ▶ from the Teleki Valley. The giant groundsels and tussock grass are typical of the moorland.

◂◂ The Curling Pond, at an altitude of 15,000 feet on Mount Kenya. Pack animals cross the frozen lake, before returning to a lower level to spend the night where grazing is available.

To obtain water, a hole had to be chopped through thick ice on the Curling Pond. Right: the permanent snowfields and glaciers of Mount Kenya are only a few miles from the equator.

Kilimanjaro, with the snow-capped summit of Kibo, forms a scenic background to a lone tusker and a herd of wilde-beest in the Masai Amboseli Game Reserve—as it does to the zebra on the following pages.

Young men from the Outward Bound Mountain School at Loitokitok are given training in leadership and teamwork while climbing Kilimanjaro. A variety of wildflowers blooms throughout the year, ranging in size from small blossoms to large flower heads of watsonia, gladioli, delphinium, protea and helichrysum.

An overnight bivouac at 19,000 feet on Kilimanjaro, looking out across a layer of clouds which hide the plains far ▸▸ below. On the following page members of the school walk around the crater rim from Gillman's Point to the summit at 19,340 feet.

Only from the air can one see the concentric circles of the crater proper. Kilimanjaro still has larger glaciers than any of the other East African mountains, but they are retreating each year. Some people believe that increased volcanic activity may be raising the temperature of the mountain. As can be seen from this aerial view the crater has a high enough temperature to prevent the build up of snow and ice.

Epilogue

In this book we have looked at life beneath the waves on the coral reef, then moved inland to the dry thornbush country, the open bush and woodland areas, and the wildlife living on the open savannah and plains country. We have studied the problems of drought, erosion, flooding and game management. We have paused to view the life associated with the fresh-water and soda lakes, which is totally different from that of the birds and mammals inhabiting the thick rain forests. Finally we have climbed the high mountains to the permanent glaciers on the roof of Africa, where everything is quiet and peaceful in the cold, rarefied air.

In looking at the wonderful wildlife which inhabits this paradise, we have only scratched the surface. Each sight, each sound, each faint scent carried on the wind is transient, but a photograph can capture the impression of a moment. After that, it is up to each person looking at the picture to interpret it. Although this is a large book, it cannot tell the full story of wildlife in Africa, or properly convey the experiences of being there. But if it brings pleasure to just one person, or if it helps even a handful to think of animals with more understanding, then the purpose behind its creation will have been achieved. Perhaps too it may spark a desire in a few people to visit Africa and see for themselves what is undoubtedly "Nature's Paradise".

Two other, completely independent books are planned: one dealing with the fascinating insect life—the small game of Africa—and another book exploring the habits and family lives of the various animals, a veritable "Wealth of Wildlife".

Index